KAUSHY PATEL

PRASHAD

AT HOME

KAUSHY PATEL

PRASHAD

AT HOME

INDIAN COOKING FROM OUR VEGETARIAN KITCHEN

Photography by

MATT RUSSELL

SALT · YARD
BOOK Co.

To Mohan, my husband and best friend.
Thank you for believing in me, encouraging me and supporting
me through every step of my amazing journey. You make
me feel as warm and special today as the first time we met.

CONTENTS

INTRODUCTION 3

KAUSHY'S KITCHEN 6

PRACTICAL POINTS, TOP TIPS, AND HOW TO... 24

SPEEDY SUPPERS 30

SLOW SUPPERS 64

LIGHT LUNCHES AND LEFTOVERS 105

INDIAN FUSION 133

FEASTS, FESTIVITIES AND SWEETS 166

ALL THE EXTRAS 199

KAUSHY'S STORE CUPBOARD AND SUPPLIES 248

ACKNOWLEDGEMENTS 250

INDEX 252

INTRODUCTION

Family and community are at the heart of Indian culture, and there's no better way to bring people together than through sharing a meal. If you've read my first cookbook, you'll know just how important food has been throughout my life, from learning to cook with my grandmother in India when I was a little girl, to setting up our award-winning restaurant, Prashad, here in the UK with my husband, Mohan. It's been an incredible journey, and it makes me very proud to see the same dishes that have been passed down through the generations in my family now being served every day to our diners. I wonder what my grandmother would think of her famous *karella na reveya* (stuffed bitter melon satay, page 80) appearing on the menu. It's a long way from her farmhouse table in her rural village in north India.

Times change. People are busier, and many of us don't live as close to our families any more. But that doesn't mean we can't all enjoy eating well, and taking every opportunity we can to get together around the table with the people that are important to us. Your food should take into account your lifestyle, and it should be a reflection of how you feel. Whether you have 20 minutes or two hours, cooking is something to be enjoyed, bringing you and those you are cooking for great pleasure. I always talk about 'cooking with love', and I really do believe it's the most important ingredient you can stir into your food. If you make a meal for someone with love, you can taste it. It's full of passion, warmth and depth.

In this book I have included all the recipes we cook at home. These are the quick dishes we prepare on weekday evenings when everyone is tired after work, they are the meals we can leave to bubble away quietly while we get on with weekend chores or to take our time over when we have something to celebrate, and they are the tasty snacks we can have ready at a moment's notice for those unexpected visitors or during a particularly hungry afternoon. Eating well means paying attention to what we put into our bodies and so, although these aren't specifically healthy recipes, they are all good wholesome meals to feed our hunger as well as our soul. But, since we Gujaratis are also well known for our love of nibbles and sweets, you'll find plenty of tasty treats too. Life is all about balance after all.

You'll find that some of the recipes are a bit of a step away from the more traditional dishes served at Prashad. Many are ones that have been in my family for generations, perhaps simplified a little to make them more suitable for everyday cooking and adapted to work with ingredients we can easily pick up at the supermarket – potatoes might replace purple yam, and ground spices often take the place of fresh ones. Other recipes are entirely new, reflecting our current lifestyles and the people around us. Throughout our forty-nine happy years living in the UK, we have fully embraced British and other cultures, and this in turn has influenced the way we cook now. Since the first book came out, Mohan and I have taken a bit of a step back from the running of the restaurant, letting Bobby and his wonderful wife, Minal, take over the reins. I'm still involved in the food, of course, but now it's a real family affair! Minal brings her own take on food, and it's been wonderful to watch the menu develop. This has also allowed us to spend more time with our gorgeous granddaughter, Maitri, and I've been able to get back into the kitchen at home, creating new versions of the dishes I cooked professionally that are suitable for my busy family life. The result is this collection of reliable dishes that anyone can cook at home.

I love how the people around us shape what we eat, and that's what I hope to share with you through these recipes. I get inspiration from all around me and as our family expands, so does the menu. Minal has brought her own culinary talents to the restaurant kitchen, and this has, in turn, influenced how we cook at home. Meanwhile, our youngest son, Mayur, has launched an Indian street food and craft beer bar, Bundobust, in Leeds city centre. This new exciting venture has brought street food – something we probably had more of at the original Prashad deli – back into our kitchen. It's very exciting to see those traditional foods finding their place among current trends, and eating them takes me straight to the wonderful bustling, colourful markets I visit whenever I'm in India.

Food is adaptable and it should suit you and your life, with all its unique demands. Cook what feels right – whether that means knocking together something quick and easy on a Tuesday evening, or spending a bit more time on an indulgent celebratory feast. And be flexible: most of the recipes here are very forgiving. If you don't have quite enough of one ingredient, just try something else. These aren't recipes you need to follow to the letter. One of the greatest things about Gujarati food is that you can get huge amounts of flavour, taste and texture from some very simple ingredients. It is endlessly versatile and you can cook delicious dishes from just a few basic items in your store. Play around with the spices and find out what you like and what you think works well together. I don't take anything too seriously – what's the point, if you're not enjoying yourself? The same applies to cooking: there are no strict rules about what you should cook when; whether it's a little street food snack, or a more complex dish designed to give you a new challenge, this food tastes good any time of day or night. And I'm absolutely not averse to a few cheats here and there either – good food can often come from a toastie maker, a jar or even a bottle of ketchup! Do whatever you need to do to get some good food onto your table that you can share with those that you love.

Whether it is a quick family supper, lunch for surprise visitors, a celebratory feast or a cheeky snack on the side, I hope that you enjoy these recipes as much as my family and I have done for many years to come.

Kaushy Patel, April 2015

KAUSHY'S SPICE TIN AND SEASONINGS

❋ **ASAFETIDA / ASAFOETIDA** (*hing*) – Also known as 'devil's dung', due to its pungent, sulphurous scent. The fine yellow powder (which is actually powdered resin) is generally fried in very small quantities when making spiced oils to be used in *dhal* and other dishes to add a savoury flavour. Store in an airtight container – vital to contain the smell. Widely believed to counter flatulence, making it the perfect partner for pulses.

❋ **CARDAMOM** (*elchi* or *elaichi*) – Available as green, white (bleached) or black/brown pods or as a dried ground spice. I prefer to dry-roast and grind the seeds in a coffee grinder or using a pestle and mortar shortly before cooking for the freshest flavour. Green cardamom is the most widely used in Indian cooking (I use green cardamom pods and their seeds for all the recipes in this book), and its black seeds are used as a digestive aid and breath freshener. Brown cardamom is used in savoury dishes and in *garam masala*. Store pods away from light and moisture in a jar or airtight tin.

❋ **CAROM** (*ajmo, ajwain* or *ajowan*) – Also known as 'Bishop's weed'. The small, curved grey-green seeds resemble celery seeds or tiny cumin seeds. Usually tempered by cooking with other ingredients, eaten raw the seeds are bitter and hot enough to numb the mouth. Thought to calm flatulence and other gastric complaints, carom is often cooked with root vegetables and pulses to aid digestion.

❋ **CHAAT MASALA** – This tangy, salty, sweet and sour spice mix is widely used in northern Indian and Pakistan to flavour snacks and street food. It typically contains Indian black salt, asafetida, dried mango powder, coriander, cumin, ginger, chilli and black pepper, although as street vendors tend mix their own, the proportions of the different spices (and resulting balance of flavours) can vary substantially. Try my bhinda fries (page 223) and you'll see why we Indians love it so.

* **CHILLI** (*marcha* or *lal/hari mirch*) – There are many different types of chillies (ripe red, unripe green, large, small, fiery, mild) and they come in many different forms (fresh, dried, flaked, pickled, powdered). I use fresh green chillies from Kenya to make my *masalas*, long green chillies for stuffed chilli *bhajis*, small dried red chillies to add to *tarka* spiced oils, coarse *resam/resham patti* (Kashmiri red chilli powder) from northern India for my pickles to give them a sweeter, less fiery warmth, and medium red chilli powder pretty much everywhere else that a chilli kick is called for. I use ready-made red and green chilli sauces sometimes too, mainly in Indo-Chinese fusion dishes like chilli *paneer* (page 152) and *hakka* noodles (page 156), and also to add a kick to *sticky chilli chips* (page 225).

* **CINNAMON** (*taaj* or *dalchini*) – This spice is made from the bark of the cinnamon tree. It is widely used in main dishes, rice dishes, puddings and sweets, and is believed to help control blood sugar levels. The warm, sweet flavour of cinnamon starts to fade from the sticks after a month or two, so buy it in relatively small amounts to keep the flavour fresh and bright.

* **CLOVES** (*lerving* or *laung*) – This small, dark-brown, woody spice is made from dried unopened clove flowerbuds. Often used whole to flavour dishes during cooking and removed before serving, it is also available in powdered form. The oil has anaesthetic qualities, hence its traditional use as a toothache remedy.

* **CORIANDER** (*dhania, dhana* or *dhanna*) – Can be used as a green-leaved herb, in seed form or as a dried ground spice (you get a better flavour if you dry-roast and grind the seeds yourself in a coffee grinder or using a pestle and mortar when needed). When buying seeds, look for light green oval ones. Fresh coriander leaves are sprinkled on many of my dishes shortly before resting or serving, while the spice tends to feature in main dishes, rice dishes and pickles.

❋ **CUMIN** (*jeeru*, *jeera* or *zeera*) – Can be bought as whole seeds or ground spice (for the best flavour, I prefer to dry-roast and grind the seeds shortly before using). The most common cumin seeds are pale green or brown, with a warm, slightly bitter taste; however, you can also find smaller, sweeter black cumin seeds (*kala jeera*). Both types are purported to cure digestive complaints. Ground cumin is often mixed with ground coriander seeds to make *dhania-jeera*.

❋ **CURRY LEAVES** (*limri*, *kari* or *khadi patta*) – Used fresh or dried, these 'sweet neem' leaves add a pungent aroma and a hint of sweetness to savoury dishes, including delicious southern Indian *kopru* (curry leaf and coconut dip, page 235). They are generally added to spiced oil (*tarka*) rather than cooked directly with other ingredients. Do take care when adding fresh leaves to hot oil, as the moisture in them makes them sizzle and spit. It is a matter of personal choice whether you eat the cooked leaves or not.

❋ **FENNEL SEEDS** – These little green seeds have a sweet aniseed scent and taste, but are milder than anise. Fennel seeds often feature in Gujarati cooking and are used to flavour Diwali dishes like *bhakar vadi* (page 180). The seeds can be chewed as a natural breath freshener, while fennel tea (made by pouring boiling water on slightly crushed seeds) can help to calm an upset stomach and act as a mild diuretic.

❋ **FENUGREEK** (*methi*) – Available as a green-leaved herb (fresh or dried), seeds or crushed spice (*bardho/bardo*). For the best results, roast and crush the seeds yourself when needed. The slightly bitter, aromatic leaves are a central component in many Indian dishes and go beautifully in relishes, flatbreads and in my *methi bhaji bataka* (page 77). The seeds, which are thought to improve digestion, have a strong curry-like flavour and can be added to spiced oils or directly with other ingredients.

❋ **GARAM MASALA** – Literally 'hot mixture', this spice blend is used in many dishes and most Indian households will have their own recipe. My secret mixture contains eighteen spices, which are slow-baked for 3 days before being stone-milled. *Garam masala* generally includes roasted ground cinnamon,

GINGER

CURRY LEAVES

BAY LEAVES

TURMERIC

WHITE TURMERIC

FRESH FENUGREEK

GARLIC

MUSTARD SEEDS

CUMIN

CHAAT MASALA

INDIAN BLACK SALT

DRIED FENUGREEK
SEEDS

CAROM

CARDAMOM

ASEFETIDA

cardamom, cloves, black cumin, nutmeg and peppercorns, but if you don't fancy making your own, it can also be bought ready-made.

❋ **GARLIC** (*lasan* or *lahsun*) – Garlic is well-known as a superfood, with antifungal and antiviral properties and beneficial effects on everything from blood pressure to acne. It plays a vital role in Indian cuisine, except during periods of fasting, when our dishes need to be onion and garlic free. I soak garlic cloves in warm water for 5 minutes before I need them, as I find it makes them easier to peel.

❋ **GINGER** (*adhu* or *adrak*) – Another staple of Indian cooking, ginger is available as a fresh root or dried spice, and lends its heat and warmth to savoury dishes and sweet treats alike. Ginger infusions have long been used to treat sore throats and nausea, and a cup or two of sweet ginger tea always cheers me up. Look for firm roots with no wrinkles or spots, and store any unused ones in the fridge for up to a couple of weeks.

❋ **INDIAN BAY LEAVES** (*tej patta*) – Paler than European bay leaves, with a yellow-khaki colour and a straighter edge, these leaves of the Indian cassia tree add a spicy aroma. I use them in many biryani and other rice dishes, as well as in curries like *paneer & mattar bhurgi* (page 56), *soya & wattana keema* (page 63) and my vegetable korma (page 89). Remove from the dish before serving.

❋ **INDIAN BLACK SALT** (*sanchar, sanchal* or *kala namak*) – This black volcanic salt has a pronounced sulphurous flavour, rather like hard-boiled eggs. The salt crystals appear black but the powdered salt is actually more pinky-grey. It gets its colour from the different minerals contained in it, including iron sulphide, hence the smell. *Sanchar* is used in ayurvedic medicine to lower blood pressure and as a laxative. It features widely in many traditional Indian dishes, for example Gujarati *undhiyu* (page 182), and is a central component in *chaat masala* spice mix.

❋ **MUSTARD SEEDS** (*rai*) – There are three main varieties: black, brown and yellow/white, available as whole or split seeds, paste or powdered spice. I use the small brown mustard seeds to bring heat and flavour to spiced oils, and the split yellow seeds (*rai bhardo/bardo* or *rai na kuria*) in pickles, as they are a wonderful preservative. When added to hot oil, brown mustard seeds start to pop as they cook, making it easy to tell that they are working their magic.

✳ **PAV BHAJI MASALA POWDER** – The dish *pav bhaji* (page 68) is a speciality of the Maharashtra region of India, and the key to making a great *pav bhaji* lies in the masala spice mix. It traditionally includes red chilli, coriander, cumin, black pepper, cinnamon, cloves, cardamom, dried mango powder and fennel, although different cooks may add other spices including ginger, bay leaf, star anise, caraway, turmeric, nutmeg and/or mace to alter the flavour balance.

✳ **PEPPER** (*mari* or *kali mirch*) – You can buy sharp white, mild green, hot black or fruity pink peppercorns (although the pink ones aren't actually from the pepper plant at all), and pepper is also widely available as a dried ground spice. I use freshly ground black peppercorns in my cooking, as I find that they work best with the other spices – if possible, take the time to grind them freshly for the best aroma and flavour.

✳ **TURMERIC** (*hardar* or *haldi*) – Often used in Indian wedding and religious ceremonies for cleansing and to bring success. Available as a dried powdered yellow spice with a peppery, earthy flavour and mustardy smell, or a fresh root with golden-orange flesh. Known in medieval Europe as 'Indian saffron' and used to dye fabric, it will stain your hands and clothes yellow if you're not careful. Unpeeled fresh turmeric keeps for up to 3 weeks in the fridge. Avoid cooking it with green vegetables, as it turns them grey.

✳ **WHITE TURMERIC** (*amba haldi* or *amb halad*) – Also known as zedoary or 'mango ginger', this closely resembles root ginger. It is less common than turmeric, has a less subtle flavour (like bitter ginger) and can be difficult to find outside India and Indonesia. It adds flavour and colour to dishes but beware the staining effect of the orange juice on hands and clothes too.

KAUSHY'S INGREDIENTS

* **AGAR AGAR** – Vegetarian gelatine substitute derived from algae, also known as kanten, China grass, Japanese moss or Bengal isinglass. It has no scent and a neutral flavour, making it ideal as a base for flavoured jellies and sweets, or for making clear vermicelli to use in *saffron & ginger panna cotta* (page 165). Can also be used as a thickening agent.

* **BASMATI RICE** – Long-grained rice from northern India with a nutty flavour and fragrant aroma. Wash thoroughly but gently before cooking to remove the starchy coating, taking care not to break the grains.

* **BESAN, CHICKPEA FLOUR OR GRAM FLOUR** – Made from ground *chana dhal*, this has a nutty flavour and yellow grainy texture. Often used for batters, fritters and porridge and in Indian sweets.

* **BHINDA** – Okra, also known as ladies' fingers', is part of the mallow family. The fresh green pods can become rather slimy when cooked, so I cut and dry them for 3 hours beforehand to avoid this. The gooey glutinous juice can be used to thicken soups and sauces.

* **BITTER MELON OR BITTER GOURD** – Also known as calabash or long melon. Immature gourds are used for cooking, mature ones are dried and used as containers, originally as bottles for carrying water (hence the name). Always try a small piece of gourd while you are grating it, and don't use it if it tastes bitter, as bitter gourd juice can sometimes cause stomach problems.

* **CHANA DHAL** – Bengal gram dhal/split skinned black chickpeas. Renowned for causing flatulence, so it is often cooked with asafetida or carom to counteract this.

CHAPATTI FLOUR, ATTA OR LOHT – Wheat flour, used for making *rotlis* and other breads. Available as refined white flour or wholewheat brown flour.

CHIKOO, SAPODILLA OR CHICO FRUIT – Also known in India as the *sapota* or 'tree potato', the fruit looks rather like a smooth tennis-ball-sized potato. The flavour and texture of the yellowy-brown flesh are similar to that of a very ripe pear, but with malty caramel tones. It contains a small number of hooked black seeds that need to be removed, as they can stick in the throat.

CORNFLOUR, CORN/MAIZE FLOUR, MAKAI NO LOHT OR MAKKI KA ATTA – Fine flour made from ground maize or sweetcorn kernels. Typically used in batters and doughs.

DOSA – A thin crispy pancake, originating from southern India and made with a fermented ground rice and *urad dhal*.

FRUIT SALTS – Effervescent fruit salts (e.g. Eno or Andrews), traditionally used to relieve indigestion, can also be used as a leavening agent in yeast-free breads. My grandmother always used fruit salts in this way. If you don't have any, substitute the same quantity of baking powder (or use bicarbonate of soda in recipes where there are acidic ingredients, e.g. lemon juice or yoghurt).

GHEE – Clarified butter, much used in traditional Indian cooking either as an ingredient (e.g. in *dhal bhati* & *churma*, page 186, and Hyderabadi biryani, page 191) or to drizzle over sweet and savoury dishes when serving. Traditionally made with cow or buffalo milk butter (the latter has a higher fat content).

GREEN MANGO – Young unripe mango, used as a sour fruit in chutneys, pickles and relishes. The stone should still be soft enough to cut through.

IDLI FLOUR – This rice and lentil flour is used to make the soft *idli* pancakes (*uttapam*, page 85) or dumplings (*idli sambar*, page 88), which are traditional in southern India.

IMLI OR AMLI (TAMARIND) – The name comes from the Arabic '*tamar hindi*', meaning Indian date, which it slightly resembles in taste. I find that pressed block tamarind, consisting of ripe tamarind pod pulp (with the shell and most of the seeds removed), provides a better flavour than concentrated paste. It is used to make tamarind water, which adds a sweet-sour note to dishes (just soak the pulp in warm water for 5 minutes, then sieve). Tamarind is also an ingredient in Worcestershire and HP sauce.

✳ **JAGGERY OR GUR** – Unrefined dehydrated cane sugar juice. Used to add sweetness to curries, breads, puddings and sweets, it has a slightly caramel-like sweet flavour. If you can't get hold of any, use soft brown or demerara sugar instead.

✳ **JUVAR, JOWAR, SORGHUM FLOUR OR MILO FLOUR** – Gluten-free flour made from ground sorghum grain kernels. Suitable for coeliacs and others with gluten intolerance. Nutritionally similar to cornflour, although higher in protein and fat, it has long been used in India to make pancakes and flatbreads. I use it in *dudhi na muthiya* (page 52) and *turai patra* (page 93).

✳ **MOMRA, KURMURA OR MAMRA** – Puffed rice – a vital ingredient in many snack and street food dishes. Store in an airtight container and try to use up quickly once you have opened the packet, as it will quickly soften and lose its crispness once exposed to the air.

✳ **MUNG OR MOONG** – Whole *mung* beans. They have a khaki-green husk and are therefore also known as green gram. Need to be soaked in advance to reduce cooking time.

✳ **MUNG OR MOONG DHAL** – Yellow split, husked *mung* beans. They are easy to cook (no need to soak) and easy to digest too, so are often served to children, the elderly and the infirm – e.g. in *mung dhal* (page 73).

✳ **PANEER** – Fresh, unsalted Indian white cheese, traditionally made at home but now widely available in supermarkets and Indian stores. Firm-textured and often griddled or fried.

✳ **PAPDI LILVA, CHIKKUDU GINJALU OR INDIAN BROAD BEANS** – These plump green beans are high in protein. They can commonly be bought either tinned or frozen. I use them in my *undhiyu* (page 182).

POINTED GOURD

AGAR AGAR

BITTER GOURD

BLACK LENTILS

YAM

JAGGERY

IMLI

BOTTLE GOURD

WHITE LENTILS

CHIKOO

RED LENTILS

CHANA DHAL

* PARVAR, PARVAL, PARWAL OR POINTED GOURD –
This green or green-and-white-striped gourd grows on a vine
similar to a cucumber or courgette plant. It is a good source of
vitamins and minerals, and is used to make soups, curries,
stews, and of course my *sukhu parvar bataka* (page 82).

* PATRA – Leaves of the colocasia plant, also known as the
elephant-ear plant or cocoyam. The green arrowhead-shaped leaves
can grow up to 150cm long, although for cooking you usually need
either small (10 x 15cm) or medium leaves (20 x 20cm). Dishes
using the stuffed leaves are a Gujarati speciality. The word '*patra*'
can be used to describe other dishes made with leaf-wrapped
parcels, not just colocasia leaves, for example my *turai patra*
spinach parcel curry (page 93).

* PAUWA, PAWA OR POHA – Flattened, beaten or pounded
parboiled rice, often used in *chaat* dishes or as a form of Indian fast
food. *Pauwa* flakes are available in differing thicknesses, from thick
to fine, depending on the weight of the rollers used to flatten the rice.

* RATALU, PURPLE YAM OR VIOLET YAM – A cylindrical
root with a thick uneven skin, requiring substantial peeling to reach
the slightly sticky, sweet purple interior. My favourite vegetable.

* RICE FLOUR – Slightly grainy white flour made from ground
washed dried rice. I tend to use it in doughs and batters, but it can
also be used to thicken sauces.

* SEMOLINA, SOJI OR SOOJI – Available as coarse, medium
or fine, this pale yellow processed durum wheat flour is used in
sweet and savoury dishes.

* SEV – Crispy Indian vermicelli noodles made from chickpea
flour, used in *chaat* dishes, as a garnish or as a snack.

* SEV MOMRA OR SEV MAMRA – Indian vermicelli combined
with puffed rice. A popular snack food.

* TAPIOCA OR SABUDANA – Best known in British cooking
for its use in milky puddings, tapioca is often used in savoury dishes
in Indian cooking, for example in soothing *sabudana kichdi* (page
41) and filling *sabudana vada* (page 116).

* **TARKA OR TADKA** – Spiced oil, stirred into *dhal* or other dishes towards the end of the cooking process to bring the spices to life. Traditionally prepared by heating *ghee* and spices together in a long-handled ladle.

* **TAWA** – Shallow metal frying pan or griddle.

* **TUVAR, TOOR OR GREEN PIGEON PEAS** – Also known as congo or gungo peas, these high-protein beans (they are in fact beans, rather than peas, despite the name) can be found frozen or tinned in supermarkets specialising in Indian foods. They can be used instead of garden peas, or to make *tuvar dhokri vada* (page 120).

* **TUVAR DHAL, TOOR DHAL OR ARHAR DHAL** – Split husked dried pigeon peas or yellow lentils. The denser texture means that this requires longer soaking and/or longer cooking times than other *dhals*. Any oily coating should be thoroughly rubbed and rinsed clean before cooking.

* **URAD DHAL, URID DHAL OR BLACK GRAM** – With their black husk and white centre, these are called 'black lentils' when whole and 'white lentils' when split and husked (which is how I usually cook them).

* **URAD / URID FLOUR OR WHITE LENTIL FLOUR** – This flour, made by grinding white lentils, is widely used in southern India, mixed with rice flour to make *idlis*, *dosas* and *uttapam* pancakes. I use it to make poppadum-like *chora fari* snacks (page 177).

* **WHITE POPPY SEEDS, KHASKAHAS OR KHUSKHUS** – Like European black or grey poppy seeds and Turkish brown poppy seeds, Indian white poppy seeds can be used in sweet and savoury dishes either as an ingredient or a garnish. They add thickness and texture as well as a subtle nutty flavour.

PRACTICAL POINTS
TOP TIPS, AND HOW TO...

PRACTICAL POINTS

⁎ Everything in this book is of course completely vegetarian (I promise that even the most die-hard carnivores won't miss the meat) and many recipes are also vegan, wheat-free, onion- and garlic-free or nut-free. We have used the following notations to help you choose the ones that are right for you:

V	....	Vegan
WF	....	Wheat-free
OG	....	Onion- & garlic-free
N	....	Nut-free
HO	....	Healthy option

⁎ All the recipes are cooked on our largest gas ring at home, which is 10cm in diameter. You may need to adapt timings according to your cooker, but I will guide you through each recipe in a way that should allow you to spot intuitively when things are right.

⁎ My local Indian stores are full of great ingredients, but I realise that not everyone has a local Indian store. As a result, when my recipe calls for an unusual ingredient, I generally try to suggest an alternative in case you can't get hold of it, as there is almost always something else you can use instead. This advice applies throughout my recipes: don't feel that you always have to follow them to the letter – if it isn't possible to find an ingredient you need or if there's something you'd rather change, improvise and try an alternative (it's your meal after all). Much of the process of great cooking is trial and error – sometimes we make mistakes, and sometimes we make magic.

PREPARATION:

* Onions, garlic, carrots, etc. in ingredients lists are all peeled unless the recipe states otherwise.
* Sometimes vegetables (usually potatoes and, in one recipe, unripe bananas) are washed but not peeled because they are to be cooked in their skins – but don't worry, the recipe will make it clear when the skin is left on and when it is peeled off.
* Where the ingredient is potentially unfamiliar to you (e.g. bottle gourd, purple yam, bitter melon, turmeric root, etc.), I have included preparation instructions in the recipe.
* Sweet peppers are always deseeded, but most of the fresh chillies have their seeds left in, as I like the flavour and heat that the seeds add.
* When using fresh coriander, I trim away all but 4cm or so of the stalks and just use the leaves.

+ I tend to use fresh grated coconut in my cooking, but if you can't find any, you can generally substitute unsweetened desiccated coconut, rehydrated in warm water and drained.

+ If the recipe doesn't call for a specific sugar, feel free to use whichever type you have to hand – I tend to use granulated white sugar.

+ The oil for cooking will always be sunflower oil unless otherwise specified.

TOP TIPS

+ I use plain live set yoghurt throughout my recipes because of its tangy taste and the creamy consistency even when whisked – it holds its structure better than runny yoghurt.

+ I find that soaking garlic cloves in warm water for 5 minutes makes them easier to peel.

+ The amount of chilli in my recipes is expressed as a range, so that you can decide how much to use depending on how hot you like your food. In the restaurant and in my home cooking, I use the higher number of chillies, but that's because I eat chillies every day.

+ Chillies vary in potency depending on where they come from and the season, so try them out, then vary the quantity according to taste. Remember, you can always add more chilli – it's a lot harder to add less!

+ If you are not used to chilli heat, you may wish to deseed fresh chillies, then soak them in cold salt water for a few minutes before chopping.

- And do take care to wear gloves when cutting chillies, so that you don't risk rubbing the juice into your eyes or lips by mistake.

- The longer you rest a dish, the more the flavours will develop and mellow, and the less heat there should be from the chillies. Many of my main dishes can be rested for hours (or even made the day before) and then reheated before serving.

- Whenever possible cook with vine tomatoes, as they taste more like home-grown tomatoes.

- Washing *dhals* – I do this using my fingertips to remove any oily coating and to make sure they get a thorough clean (the water should run clear by the end). Using my hands also helps me to find and remove any small stones that may have crept in when the pulses were being sorted or packaged.

- Rinsing rice several times before cooking washes away enough starch to make sure your rice will be fluffy and loose when cooked, but do take care not to break the grains, as this will make it more (rather than less) starchy.

- I find that mixing a marinade with my hands helps the combination of spices to come alive.

- Have a go at grinding your own spices, rather than buying them ready-ground – you will find the flavours much more intense. When a recipe calls for ground cardamom seeds, for example, gently crush a few green cardamom pods and extract the little round black seeds. Then grind these in an electric coffee/spice grinder or crush using a pestle and mortar for wonderfully fragrant ground cardamom. Some spices like cumin seeds require roasting before you grind them, but it's very simple to do – see my How To tips box.

- I always use a wooden spoon when frying spices because I feel that the natural material allows the love to flow out of my fingers and into my food. If you don't have one, use a heatproof plastic or silicone spoon instead.

- Where a recipe calls for thawed peas (usually pigeon peas or petits pois), I do this by soaking them in warm water for 15–20 minutes, then draining.

- Sometimes when making *bread bhajia* (page 111) you may have some batter left over. Rather than waste it, cut a potato (washed but not peeled) into 5mm-thick slices, then batter and fry to make crispy *kakra bhajia* (page 221).

- Try not to cook when you are stressed or short of time – cooking should be a pleasure as well as a means to an end. And always think beautiful thoughts while you cook. Not only will it make you feel happier, but it makes your food taste beautiful too.

HOW TO ...

HOW TO ...
ROAST CUMIN SEEDS

Dry-roast the cumin seeds in a frying pan over a low heat for about
2 minutes, shaking the pan to toast them evenly, until they start to darken
slightly. Set aside to cool, then just before you need to add the spice to your
dish, use a pestle and mortar or a blender to crush the seeds finely.
A tablespoon of seeds will yield about 4–5 teaspoons of ground cumin.

HOW TO ...
STOP CHOPPED AUBERGINE OR POTATO
FROM OXIDIZING

When cutting aubergines or potatoes in advance, put the
pieces into a bowl of water as soon as you've cut them. Drain
when you're ready to cook them.

HOW TO ...
STOP YOUR *DHAL* PAN FOAMING OVER

Once the *dhal* starts to foam, skim the froth from the top and
add a teaspoon of oil to the water to stop it bubbling up.

HOW TO ...
PREVENT *TARKA* SPICES FROM BURNING

When making a *tarka* spiced oil, reduce the heat as soon as the seeds start to brown, as they will continue to cook in the hot oil.

HOW TO ...
PICK AND PREPARE FRESH COCONUT

When buying fresh coconuts, look for ones with plenty of water in them (give them a good shake) and no mildew on the 'eyes'. To open, use a skewer to punch holes through the eyes and drain out the coconut water – it makes a delicious refreshing drink. Use a hammer to crack open the shell, prise out the coconut 'meat', use a vegetable peeler to remove the brown skin, then grate. You can freeze any you don't need – frozen grated coconut will keep for up to 3 months.

HOW TO ...
ADD MOIST INGREDIENTS TO HOT OIL SAFELY

Always reduce the heat before adding anything that contains moisture (e.g. chopped onion or fresh curry leaves) to hot oil, as the water will cause the oil to spit on contact and if it catches you, it can cause nasty burns. Just add, stand well back and enjoy the sizzle.

HOW TO ...
BALANCE CHILLI-HOT FOOD

Yoghurty dishes and sweet dishes will temper the fire from chillies. Serve a yoghurt dip or mango *lassi* with your meal to cool the taste buds, or try having a little something sweet after a particularly hot mouthful – you'll be amazed at the difference it can make.

SPEEDY SUPPERS

RENGHAN LOTHIU · spicy fried aubergines

KOBI PURA · cabbage pancakes

SABZHI RASSA · mixed vegetable soup

DHUDI BATAKA RASSA · creamy marrow & potato soup

MUMBAI SANDWICH · spiced potato & pea toastie

SABUDANA KICHDI · spiced savoury tapioca

SAKABHAJI UPMA · savoury Indian porridge

TAMETA REVEYA · vine tomato satay

BATAKA TAMETA · potato & tomato curry

KHANDA BATAKA · potato & onion curry

FANSI · tomato, carom and French bean curry

DUDHI NA MUTHIYA · bottle gourd and coriander dumplings

LASAN BHAJI · fenugreek- and garlic-infused spinach curry

PANEER & MATTAR BHURGI · shredded *paneer* curry

SUKHU KOBI WATTANA · cabbage & pea curry

SHIMLA MAKAI · pepper & sweetcorn curry

RAJMA · classic Punjabi-style kidney bean curry

CHORA · black-eyed bean curry

SOYA & WATTANA KEEMA · soya mince & pea curry

We all know that modern life can be incredibly hectic at times, and nowdays most of us simply don't have the luxury of spending hours preparing an evening meal. But I think being so busy means it's even more important to eat well, and to make precious time for one another around the dinner table as often as we can.

One of the beautiful aspects of Gujarati cuisine is that it uses fresh, colourful ingredients that pack a real flavour punch without too much effort on your part. Being vegetable-based, many of the dishes can be cooked very quickly, which has the added bonus of retaining more of their goodness and wonderful unique qualities. You can get all the taste and texture without fussing around with lengthy infusing, marinating, boiling and baking. Traditionally, in Indian households, whoever was in charge of the cooking was responsible for providing nutritious meals for their families every day. They needed a huge amount of creativity, working with the often rather limited selection of ingredients on offer, most of which would just be growing in their back gardens or in the neighbouring fields. This has resulted in an amazingly diverse range of dishes, based on simple produce that can be served up to satisfy hungry families night after night. Just what we all need today! Maybe times aren't so different after all.

The recipes in this chapter are very relaxed. Whilst I love spending time pulling together a complex feast, there's also something very satisfying – and fun – about putting a filling, delicious meal on the table very quickly. These are the truly homely dishes that my children remember fondly from their childhoods and now regularly cook themselves. They are often based on classic recipes that have been adapted to fit into our lifestyles, maybe making use of leftovers or a more convenient cooking technique – you'll find fast curries, soups, and there's even a toastie. I often make some of the elements that would usually be served up as part of a larger feast menu but, rather than making two or three (and often many more) items to share around the table, in this chapter I've suggested some simply cooked rice or a pile of breads to eat alongside instead. And there are, of course, some of my favourite street food snacks. Cooking and eating quickly doesn't mean we should forget how to eat properly – we just need to make a few adjustments along the way and be flexible, which is, essentially, what life is all about.

Be confident in the kitchen and enjoy the freedom these recipes offer you. Experiment with different variations and make these meals work for you and your lifestyle.

RENGHAN LOTHIU ~ spicy fried aubergines

(V, WF, OG, N, HO)

If I'm honest, these rarely make it onto the dinner table, as everyone usually crowds around the pan waiting to grab them as soon as they are ready! They are shallow-fried, so they make a great hot snack, slightly healthier than a deep-fried version, and they work really well as part of a selection of sharing plates or a starter for a bigger feast. For a quick mid-week meal, though, I serve them with the simple fluffy tomato rice on page 211 and plenty of cooling sour cream.

SERVES 4

175g gram (chickpea) flour, sieved
1½ tsp medium red chilli powder
3 tsp salt
1 tsp turmeric
1 tsp cumin seeds
¼ tsp asafetida
2 tsp ground coriander
½ tsp ground cumin
100ml sunflower oil
2 large aubergines, washed,
  sliced in circular 1cm-wide discs,
  and soaked in water with 1 tsp salt
1 handful fresh coriander,
  washed and finely chopped

Put the flour, chilli powder, salt, turmeric, cumin seeds, asafetida, ground coriander and ground cumin into a large mixing bowl and, making sure your hands are dry, mix everything together by hand.

Heat the oil for 1 minute in a large, thick-based frying pan. Taking a slice of aubergine out of the soaking water, shake off any excess and then dab each side in the spiced flour. Place the well-coated aubergine in the pan and repeat until the pan is full. This should take about 3 minutes and you should have coated around half the slices.

Fry the coated aubergine slices on a medium heat for a minute, then gently turn each one and fry on the other side for 3 minutes. Turn again and fry for 5 minutes. Turn once more, cover and cook for 4 minutes. Gently remove from the pan and place on a serving plate.

Repeat the process with the remaining slices. By now the spiced flour will be getting quite sticky, so just smear it onto the aubergines if dabbing is not feasible.

Once all the slices have been cooked, serve immediately on a bed of *tameta pilau* (page 211) with a generous dollop of sour cream.

KOBI PURA & cabbage pancakes

(N, HO)

An authentic Gujarati recipe using ingredients easily available in most rural Indian kitchens, these pancakes would traditionally have been made as part of a larger spread of dishes, but now I cook them as a quick mid-week meal. The batter is very forgiving, so experiment with different vegetables – kale, finely sliced carrots, peas and even cooked sweet potato will all work well. The only real rule I insist on is to enjoy them while they are still sizzling, straight from the pan, and while your kitchen is full of their smoky delicious aromas.

SERVES 4

Masala
4–6 fresh green chillies (ideally Kenyan)
2–4 cloves of garlic, soaked and peeled
4cm root ginger, peeled
pinch of salt

400g white cabbage, washed and finely sliced (approx. ½cm x 5cm)
220g sorghum flour, sieved
60g chapatti flour, sieved
175g plain live set yoghurt
2½ tsp salt
1½ tsp sugar
3½ tsp ground coriander
½ tsp ground cumin
1 tsp turmeric
1 tsp cumin seeds
1 handful fresh coriander, washed and finely chopped
400ml water
50ml sunflower oil

Crush the chillies, garlic and ginger together with a pinch of salt using a pestle and mortar (or a blender), to make a fine masala paste.

Put the cabbage, sorghum flour, chapatti flour, yoghurt, salt, sugar, ground coriander, ground cumin, turmeric, cumin seeds and fresh coriander in a large, deep mixing bowl. Mix everything together, working the spices and flour into the cabbage with your fingers and thumbs. Initially add 200ml water and gently mix everything together. Add the rest of the water and combine with your hands using a more whisk-like motion, agitating the batter to make sure all the flour has been incorporated and the spices have fully infused the runny batter. Taste and season to your liking.

Heat a frying pan on a medium heat for 1½ minutes, then add 1 teaspoon of sunflower oil and a full ladle of batter. Using the back of a spoon, spread the batter into a circular shape, approximately 16cm in diameter. Cook for 1½ minutes or until the *pura* is flippable. Flip over and fry for 3 minutes. Flip again and fry for a further 2 minutes on each side.

The traditional Indian way is to eat this on its own with some jaggery shavings on the side, however I like to serve it piping hot with vagarela beans (page 136) to the person who is most likely to do the washing up first. Repeat until everyone is full.

SABZHI RASSA ~ mixed vegetable soup

(V, WF, OG, N, HO)

At my grandmother's home in India, early every morning people would come to the door with baskets of fresh vegetables for sale: aubergines, tomatoes, fresh chillies, spinach... whatever was in season. These ingredients would be the basis for the day's meals. In a similar way, this soup is great for using up what you already have – the odd ends of vegetables lurking in your fridge. Perhaps not quite as romantic as people coming to the door with baskets of produce, but I like to think the same sentiment is there! If you don't polish it off in one sitting, the soup will keep in the fridge for up to a week, for whenever anyone fancies another bowlful.

SERVES 4

4 tsp cornflour, sieved
50ml cold water
30ml sunflower oil
1 tsp cumin seeds
1 large carrot, peeled and cut in
  1cm dice
½ medium courgette, cut in 1cm dice
½ medium red pepper, cut in
  1cm dice
6 baby sweetcorn, cut in 1cm dice
80g broccoli, cut in 1cm dice
1 large vine tomato, cut in 1cm dice
3 fresh green chillies (ideally
  Kenyan), finely chopped
½ tsp ground black pepper
2 tsp salt
¼ tsp turmeric
1 handful fresh coriander,
  washed and finely chopped
1.2 ltr boiling water

Mix the cornflour with the cold water in a small bowl. Make sure that all of it has dissolved, then leave to one side.

Heat the oil in a large thick-based pan for 2 minutes over a medium heat, then add the cumin seeds and swirl through the warm oil. As soon as the seeds start to froth, add the carrot, mix through the oil and fry for 1 minute. Stir in the courgettes and fry for 1 minute, then stir in the pepper and fry for another minute or so until the vegetables have started to soften. Stir in the baby sweetcorn and broccoli and fry for a further 2 minutes, stirring occasionally to help the cumin oil really infuse the vegetables.

Stir in the tomato and cook covered for 2 minutes before stirring again and adding the green chillies, black pepper, salt, turmeric, and fresh coriander. Mix through and leave to cook uncovered for 1 minute. Now stir in the boiling water along with the cornflour paste to thicken everything up. Turn the heat to high and bring to a simmer whilst stirring. Simmer for 6 minutes, then take off the heat and leave to rest covered, allowing the flavours to develop.

I serve this warm after 5 minutes without the need to reheat again, but if you have made this dish in advance, bring it back to the boil before serving. This soup is best eaten just as it is, with warm crusty bread.

DHUDI BATAKA RASSA ⟨ creamy marrow & potato soup

(V, WF, N)

35g salted butter

1 tsp carom seeds

¼ tsp asafetida

1 large marrow, peeled and
  cut in 1cm dice

2 medium red-skinned
  (or other waxy) potatoes, peeled
  and cut in 1cm dice

2 fresh green chillies (ideally
  Kenyan), finely chopped

2–3 cloves of garlic, soaked
  and finely chopped

½ tsp ground black pepper

2 tsp salt

650ml boiling water

4 tbsp fresh cream, to serve

Marrow and potato is a match made in heaven. In India there is a huge range of marrows, courgettes and squashes in all sorts of colours and sizes – small round yellow ones, white ones, long thin ones, some that are squashed almost flat. They're beautiful to see piled up in the kitchen, and I remember them appearing in lots of meals during their harvest season. There's not quite the same variety in the UK, but if you see a lovely yellow courgette, or a bright-looking pumpkin – or really, any type of squash – use it in this rich, thick soup.

Melt the butter in a large thick-based pan on a low heat for 3 minutes, then add the carom seeds and asafetida. Swirl the spices through and heat for 30 seconds, allowing the carom seeds just enough time to infuse the butter. Add the marrow and potatoes and stir everything together. Cook uncovered for 2 minutes to allow the spices to work into the vegetables.

Add the green chillies, garlic, black pepper, salt and 200ml of the boiling water, mix everything together and cook on a medium heat for 5 minutes. Pour in the remaining boiling water, give everything a good stir, cover and leave to cook for about 30 minutes.

Take off the heat and blitz to a thick, smooth texture (I use a stick blender). Season to taste. Serve immediately in big bowls, finishing each with a table-spoon of fresh cream.

MUMBAI SANDWICH ~ spiced potato & pea toastie

(V, OG, N, HO)

A perfect example of the culinary magic that can occur when British and Indian cultures combine. These filling and nutritious toasties take the basis for a classic Indian spiced side dish and envelop it in slices of warm doughy bread. If you don't have a toastie maker, fry them in a hot dry pan until golden brown on both sides. Press down firmly with a spatula while frying to give even contact with the hot surface, and to help seal the sides together before you carefully turn them over.

SERVES 4

16 slices of bread, crusts removed
butter

Masala
6–8 fresh green chillies
  (ideally Kenyan)
4cm root ginger, peeled
pinch of salt

Filling
75ml sunflower oil
2 tsp cumin seeds
2 medium potatoes, peeled and
  cut in 1cm dice
200g frozen petits pois peas,
  thawed
1 medium carrot, peeled and
  cut in 1cm dice
1½ tsp salt
pinch of turmeric
1 handful fresh coriander,
  washed and finely chopped
1 medium vine tomato,
  washed and cut in 1cm dice

Crush the chillies and ginger together with a pinch of salt using a pestle and mortar (or a blender), to make a fine masala paste.

Heat the oil in a large thick-based frying pan for 2 minutes over a medium heat. Add the cumin seeds and swirl through the oil. Once they start to froth, mix in the potatoes, peas and carrot and cook for 30 seconds. Now add the masala paste, salt, turmeric and coriander. Mix through, then cover and cook for 8 minutes, stirring halfway though. Stir in the tomato, re-cover and cook for a further 2 minutes, then take off the heat and leave to rest, still covered, allowing all the flavours to come together. Butter one side of each slice of bread.

Preheat your toastie maker, then carefully place a piece of bread buttered-side down on the heated base plate. Heap on a generous amount of filling and cover with another slice of bread, this time buttered-side up. Make as many as your toastie maker can cook at once, toasting for 5–6 minutes or until the bread is crisp and golden. Serve piping hot with *bhinda* fries (page 223).

SABUDANA KICHDI ⟨ spiced savoury tapioca

(V, WF, OG, HO)

My son Bobby's wife, Minal, has always dreamed of running a restaurant, ever since she was a little girl, and now she does! I can't believe how lucky we are to have her join the family; it's a match made by the gods. This is one of Minal's all-time favourite home-cooked dishes and I love making it for her. Eat it as soon as it is ready, as the longer you leave it, the stickier and stodgier it becomes. There are many fasting days within our religious calendar and this tapioca kichdi is very popular during these times because of its slow-releasing energy.

SERVES 4

290g tapioca
300ml warm water, for soaking
60ml sunflower oil
2 tsp cumin seeds
2 medium red-skinned (or other waxy) potatoes, peeled and cut in 1cm dice
7cm root ginger, peeled and blended to a pulp
8 fresh green chillies (ideally Kenyan), finely chopped (not blended)
2 tsp salt
100g red-skinned (unroasted, unsalted) peanuts, finely chopped or blended
1 handful fresh coriander, washed and finely chopped, to garnish
1 fresh lemon, quartered

Soak the tapioca in the warm water for 10–12 minutes.

Warm the oil in a thick-based pan for 2 minutes. Add the cumin seeds and swirl through the oil. When the cumin seeds start to gently froth, mix in the potatoes and cook covered for 3 minutes. Add the ginger, green chillies, salt and peanuts. Mix everything through, making sure the spices infuse throughout, and cook covered for 1 minute. Now turn the heat to low and cook covered for 6 minutes, making sure you stir and scrape the bottom of the pan every 2 minutes.

Drain the tapioca. Check the potatoes are cooked, then add the tapioca and stir through. Cover and cook for 4–5 minutes, giving it a good stir every minute or so. You will notice the stirring is becoming much harder, but persevere with it.

Garnish with the coriander and serve immediately in large bowls with a good squeeze of fresh lemon and *chana chaat patti* (page 244).

SAKABHAJI UPMA ⟨ savoury Indian porridge

(V, N, HO)

Like the paneer bhurji *on page 56, this porridge would traditionally be served for breakfast in India, but I think it works much better as a warming supper on a cold wintery British evening. It is actually a South Indian dish, but I've given it a few telltale Gujarati twists with some extra veggies, spices and fresh herbs. Single-bowl meals like this are perfect for speedy suppers – and there's less washing up too…*

SERVES 4

50ml sunflower oil

2 tsp cumin seeds

½ tsp asafetida

10–12 fresh curry leaves, washed

½ medium onion, peeled and cut
   in ½cm dice

1 medium carrot, peeled and cut
   in 1cm dice

1 medium red pepper, cut in 1cm dice

100g frozen petits pois peas,
   thawed

5cm root ginger, peeled and blended
   to a pulp

4–6 fresh green chillies (ideally
   Kenyan), finely chopped (not
   blended)

½ tsp turmeric

2 tsp salt

2 handfuls fresh coriander,
   washed and finely chopped,
   plus extra to garnish

215g fine semolina

800ml boiling water

olive oil, to serve

Heat the oil in a large, deep, thick-based frying pan for 2 minutes on a medium heat. Add the cumin seeds and swirl in the oil. Once they start to gently froth, stir in the asafetida. Now add the curry leaves at arm's length and enjoy the lovely lemony sizzle for a moment before stirring in the onion and cooking uncovered for 1 minute. Stir in the carrot and cook for a further 2 minutes, then finally stir in the pepper and cook for 2 minutes more.

Once all the hard vegetables have started to soften, add the peas, ginger, green chillies, turmeric, salt and 1 handful of fresh coriander. Gently mix all the spices through and cook uncovered for 1½ minutes, helping all the flavours to develop. Now add the semolina and 600ml of boiling water. Carefully stir everything together, folding the semolina and water through the vegetables, and cook for 1 minute. Turn the heat to low and cook for a further minute, then add the remaining 200ml of boiling water. Stir and cook covered for 30 seconds.

Serve straight away in large bowls with a drizzle of olive oil, a sprinkle of fresh coriander and some *barela marcha* (page 243).

TAMETA REVEYA ୧ vine tomato satay

(V, WF, HO)

This sweet and spicy satay is one of my own creations and it has made many regular appearances on the Patel dining table over the years. It demonstrates how easy it is to elevate everyday ingredients into something to celebrate with just a few carefully balanced spices, which lies at the heart of all Gujarati cooking. For a more substantial dinner, I often serve these as a topping for a good old baked potato.

SERVES 4

Masala

1–3 fresh green chillies (ideally Kenyan), trimmed but not de-seeded

2–4 cloves of garlic, soaked and peeled

4cm root ginger, peeled and roughly chopped

pinch of salt

150g red-skinned (unroasted, unsalted) peanuts, finely chopped or blended

25g jaggery, cut in thin flakes (or demerara / soft brown sugar)

3½ tsp ground coriander

½ tsp ground cumin

2 tsp turmeric

1½ tsp salt

1 tsp cumin seeds

½ tsp asafetida

1 tsp medium red chilli powder

2 handfuls fresh coriander, washed and finely chopped

100ml sunflower oil

9 medium vine tomatoes, washed

350ml boiling water

Crush the chillies, garlic and ginger together with a pinch of salt using a pestle and mortar (or a blender), to make a fine masala paste.

Put the peanuts, jaggery, ground coriander, ground cumin, turmeric, salt, cumin seeds, asafetida, chilli powder, masala paste and 1 handful of fresh coriander into a large mixing bowl. Pour the sunflower oil over the top. Using your hands, mix everything through, working the spices in. Whilst you are rubbing the marinade between your fingers and thumbs, the jaggery will start to melt and create small spice-infused pockets. Leave to rest for 5 minutes.

Whilst the marinade is resting, partially cut the tomatoes into quarters from the base, leaving the last couple of centimetres at the stem-end intact so that the tomatoes hold together. Gently prise them open and spread a generous quantity of marinade onto the cut surfaces. Be sure to spread it right to the end of the incisions but take care not to overfill them, as the tomatoes may split apart completely. This process ensures that the marinade fully infuses the tomatoes during cooking. If some of your tomatoes split, spread the marinade on the cut side before adding to the pan.

Arrange the filled tomatoes in a large pan facing up and drop any remaining marinade evenly between them. Place on a medium heat. Wash the marinade off your hands and into the marinade bowl using

CONTINUED OVERLEAF

the hot water. Scrape all the marinade from the sides of the bowl, then stir into the warm water, making sure you don't waste any of the flavour. Once the tomatoes start to sizzle, gently pour this diluted marinade goodness into the gaps between them. Cover and cook for 6 minutes.

Very gently turn the tomatoes, then cover again and cook for a further 10 minutes. Take off the heat and leave to rest for 10 minutes to allow the flavours to develop. You may wonder why we have been so careful with the tomatoes throughout the process, since they will now have fallen apart, but I find that this slow breakdown allows the marinade to work its magic, adding a wonderful, rich taste.

Reheat over a medium heat, garnish with the remaining coriander and serve with *jeera baath* (page 214) or *tuvar pilau* (page 212).

BATAKA TAMETA ⟨ potato & tomato curry

(V, WF, N, HO)

Cumin and mustard seeds bring a prominent earthiness to this dish and the tomatoes provide the all-important sauce – which I recommend you scoop up with plenty of rotli breads (see page 206). This is a real taste of India that can be easily achieved as a quick and much healthier alternative to a takeaway.

SERVES 4

100ml sunflower oil
2 tsp cumin seeds
1 tsp mustard seeds
¼ tsp asafetida
4 medium red-skinned (or other waxy) potatoes, peeled and cut in 1cm cubes
3½ tsp ground coriander
½ tsp ground cumin
2 tsp salt
1 tsp sugar
1 tsp turmeric
2½ tsp medium red chilli powder
2 handfuls fresh coriander, washed and finely chopped
4–5 medium vine tomatoes, washed and cut in 2cm dice, keeping all the juices
225ml boiling water

Heat the oil in a large thick-based frying pan over a medium heat for 2 minutes. Add the cumin seeds and swirl through the oil, then, as soon as they start to froth, add the mustard seeds. Once the mustard seeds start to pop, reduce the heat to low and stir in the asafetida.

Add the potatoes, stir through and cook uncovered for 1 minute. Keep stirring and, once all the potatoes are coated in the infused oil, stir in the ground coriander, ground cumin, salt, sugar, turmeric, chilli powder and 1 handful of fresh coriander. Cover and cook for 8 minutes, giving everything a good stir halfway through. Mix in the tomatoes and boiling water, turn the heat up to medium, bring to a simmer and cook covered for 6–7 minutes. Now check the potatoes: they should be lovely and soft; if not, cook for a further 1–2 minutes.

Remove from the heat and leave to rest covered for at least 10 minutes to allow the flavours to infuse.

Reheat over a medium heat until piping hot, then sprinkle with the remaining fresh coriander and serve with *tuvar pilau* (page 212) and/or *mitu gajar murabho* (page 233).

KHANDA BATAKA ❧ potato & onion curry

(V, WF, N, HO)

The real secret to quick cooking is to work with what you have. This curry uses ingredients that you will probably already have at home – or if not, they are very easily picked up on the way back from work. It is the spices that do all the hard work here, bringing warm flavours to the humble potato. My husband, Mohan, absolutely loves potatoes and always gives a little extra smile when he smells this being cooked.

SERVES 4

Masala
4–6 fresh green chillies (ideally Kenyan), trimmed but not de-seeded
4cm root ginger, peeled and roughly chopped
pinch of salt

100ml sunflower oil
2 tsp mustard seeds
½ tsp asafetida
3 medium onions, peeled and cut in 2cm dice
4–5 medium red-skinned (or other waxy) potatoes, peeled and cut in ½cm dice
½ tsp turmeric
2½ tsp ground coriander
¼ tsp ground cumin
2 tsp salt
1 tsp sugar
2 handfuls fresh coriander, washed and finely chopped

Crush the chillies and ginger together with a pinch of salt using a pestle and mortar (or a blender), to make a fine masala paste.

Heat the oil in a large thick-based frying pan over a medium heat for 2 minutes. Add the mustard seeds and swirl through the oil. Listen out for the seeds starting to pop, then reduce the heat to low and stir in the asafetida.

Use a wooden or heatproof plastic spoon to stir in the onions and potatoes, giving them a good mix through. Cover and cook for 1 minute. Now stir in the masala paste, turmeric, ground coriander, ground cumin, salt, sugar, and 1 handful of fresh coriander. Turn up to medium heat, stir through and cook covered for 15 minutes or so, stirring halfway through. Once the potatoes are soft, remove from the heat and leave to rest covered for at least 10 minutes to allow the flavours to infuse.

Reheat over a medium heat until piping hot, then sprinkle with the remaining fresh coriander and serve with *makai rotla* (page 202) and/or *tuvar dhal kichdi* (page 217).

FANSI ⟨ tomato, carom and French bean curry

(V, WF, OG, N, HO)

*Mohan loves yoga and tries to live by the traditional Vedic principles.
This means he's always telling us about natural remedies for any ailments
we have. French beans are known within Indian culture for keeping
blood sugar levels under control, making this a good dish for anyone
with a sweet tooth – like me!*

SERVES 4

Masala
4–6 fresh green chillies (ideally
  Kenyan), trimmed but not
  de-seeded
3cm root ginger, peeled and
  roughly chopped
pinch of salt

450g French beans
125ml sunflower oil
3 tsp carom seeds
¼ tsp asafetida
2 tsp turmeric
2 tsp salt
2 tsp ground coriander
½ tsp ground cumin
2 medium vine tomatoes,
  chopped or blended to
  a coarse pulp
2 handfuls fresh coriander,
  washed and finely chopped

Crush the chillies and ginger together with a pinch
of salt using a pestle and mortar (or a blender),
to make a fine masala paste. Rinse the beans, remove
the strings from along their seams and cut in half
across the middle.

Heat the oil in a large thick-based pan for 2 minutes
over a medium heat, then add the carom seeds and
fry for no more than 30 seconds before adding
the asafetida and French beans. The pan is likely to
be very full, so turn the beans carefully, ensuring they
are all lightly coated with oil, then let them sizzle
gently while you add the masala paste, turmeric, salt,
ground coriander and ground cumin. Stir through,
cover and cook on a medium heat for 7 minutes,
stirring every few minutes. Stir in the tomatoes and
half the fresh coriander, re-cover, reduce the heat to
low and cook for a further 7 minutes.

Remove from the heat, sprinkle with the remaining
fresh coriander and leave to rest covered for at least
10 minutes to allow the flavours to infuse.

Reheat over a low heat until piping hot and serve
with *makai rotla* (page 202).

DUDHI NA MUTHIYA ❧ bottle gourd and coriander dumplings

(WF, N, HO)

When I was little, my grandma would make this for me whenever I was feeling poorly and had to stay in bed; she would say that the deep flavours would wake up my taste buds. The steamy dumplings are cooked quickly to carefully preserve all their goodness, and they're very easy to eat. It's a simple, soothing dish; perfect for when your spirits need rousing. (Not that I would openly condone this, but this also makes a great mess-free TV dinner!) It's just the kind of simple, restorative food you need if you're having a busy week.

NOTE: *While you are grating the gourd, taste a little piece. If it is bitter, don't use it, as bitter gourd juice can give you a stomachache. If you can't get hold of bottle gourd, cabbage makes a good substitute. I make my own steamer to cook the* muthiya *but you can use a plate in a regular steamer if you have one.*

SERVES 4

Masala
4–6 fresh green chillies (ideally
  Kenyan), trimmed but not de-seeded
4–6 cloves of garlic, soaked
  and peeled
4cm root ginger, peeled
pinch of salt

Dough
125g sorghum flour, sieved
90g gram (chickpea) flour, sieved
2 medium (approx. 530g) bottle
  gourd, peeled and coarsely blended
50ml sunflower oil
25g plain live set yoghurt (optional)
3½ tsp ground coriander
½ tsp ground cumin
pinch of turmeric
1½ tsp salt
2 tsp sugar (optional)
1 handful fresh coriander,
  washed and finely chopped
approx. 75ml water

olive oil, to serve

Crush the chillies, garlic and ginger together with a pinch of salt using a pestle and mortar (or a blender), to make a fine masala paste.

Mix both the sieved flours together well in a large, deep bowl. Tip in the coarsely-blended gourd along with any juice it has released. Now add the masala paste and all the remaining dough ingredients apart from the water. Mix all the ingredients together. Take your time and make sure all the spices are mixed through. Gradually add water little by little until you have a sticky dough – you need to be able to shape the mixture, so don't add too much water or the dough won't hold its form. 75ml should be perfect, but this may vary slightly, as different batches of flour vary in absorption rates.

Create a makeshift steamer in which to cook the *muthiya* by putting a flat-based steel or china bowl upside-down in a large, deep pan. Pour water into the pan until most of the bowl is covered, leaving about 1cm sticking above the water, and place the pan over a high heat.

Lightly oil a plate that will fit in the pan – use a plate with a 2cm rim or lip, so that you have something to grip when removing it from the steamer, and so that the *muthiya* don't fall into the water while you're doing so. Take a small handful of the dough, gently form into a sausage or kebab shape and place on the oiled plate. As your hands get sticky, dip them in water. Repeat until all the dough is used up. Gently place the filled plate on top of the inverted bowl in the pan. Put the lid on the pan, wrap the rim of the lid with a cloth or tea towel and (if it is a flat lid) put a weight on the lid to secure it. Reduce the heat to medium, and then leave the *muthiya* to cook for 20 minutes.

Carefully remove the plate from the makeshift steamer and leave to cool for 5 minutes. Gently spoon the *muthiya* onto a serving plate and drizzle with a little olive oil before serving.

LASAN BHAJI   ❬   fenugreek- and garlic-infused spinach curry

(V, WF, HO)

*Spinach is a great base for a healthy midweek supper because it is so quick
and easy to cook. I cut it into strips the day before making this dish because it
helps to dry out some of the moisture in the leaves, but you can skip this step
if you prefer a more liquid sauce. I love starting with so much spinach that
it seems impossible to fit in the pan and then watching as it miraculously wilts
into a flavoursome, gooey sauce.*

SERVES 4

100ml sunflower oil

2 tsp fenugreek seeds

½ tsp asafetida

6 cloves of garlic, soaked, peeled
and cut into 2mm discs

1kg fresh leaf spinach, washed,
cut into 1cm strips and left to
dry overnight

2 medium onions, peeled and sliced
into 5mm strips

2 tsp salt

1 tsp turmeric

3 tsp ground coriander

1 tsp ground cumin

1½ tsp medium red chilli powder

Heat the oil in a large thick-based pan for 2 minutes
over a medium heat. Add the fenugreek seeds and
swirl through the warm oil; they will start to darken
within seconds. Now stir in the asafetida and garlic,
and fry until the garlic starts to brown – this should
take approximately 30 seconds.

Add half the spinach (which will seem like tons),
cover and cook for 3 minutes. During this time the
spinach will have wilted, making space in your pan
for the remaining spinach and the onions. Gently
stir through, cover again and cook for 4 minutes.

Mix everything through, which will be easier now
that all the spinach has wilted. Add the salt, turmeric,
ground coriander, ground cumin and chilli powder,
gently stirring through, and cook uncovered for
4 minutes.

Serve immediately with *tuvar dhal kichdi* (page 217)
and *khudi* (page 226).

PANEER & MATTAR BHURGI <small>&</small> shredded *paneer* curry

(V, WF, N, HO)

In India, paneer bhurgi *is enjoyed for breakfast, a bit like scrambled eggs. Hearty breakfasts were essential for the farmers who would be working in the fields from dawn until midday, when they'd take a well-earned break from the hot sun. My grandmother's family were all farmers, and every morning she used to make breakfast for all of their workers – usually more than 200 hungry men to feed! For most of us, this is probably a bit rich for breakfast, so I now serve it with a little cooked rice as a wholesome easy evening meal.*

SERVES 4

Masala
4–6 cloves of garlic, soaked and
  peeled
4cm root ginger, peeled
pinch of salt

75ml sunflower oil
1 large Indian bay leaf, washed
3cm cinnamon stick
3 cloves
1 tsp cumin seeds
1½ medium onions, cut in ½cm
  dice
3 medium vine tomatoes, cut in
  1cm dice
1 tsp turmeric
2 tsp medium red chilli powder
1¾ tsp ground coriander
¼ tsp ground cumin
2 tsp salt
2 tsp *garam masala*
2 handfuls fresh coriander,
  washed and finely chopped
100g frozen peas, thawed
150ml warm water
360g *paneer* cheese, grated

Crush the garlic and ginger together with a pinch of salt using a pestle and mortar (or a blender), to make a fine masala paste.

Heat the oil in a large thick-based frying pan for 2 minutes and add the bay leaf, cinnamon, cloves and cumin seeds. Gently swirl the spices through the warm oil and leave on a medium heat for 30 seconds to help it infuse with the rich warm flavours. Stir in the onions and cook uncovered for 3 minutes. Now turn up the heat to full and cook the onions for a further 3 minutes, stirring regularly to make sure they do not stick and burn on the bottom of the pan.

Stir in the tomatoes and cook for 3 minutes, then turn the heat back to medium, cover and cook for 3 minutes. The juices from the tomatoes will help the spices mix into the sauce. Now add the masala paste, turmeric, chilli powder, ground coriander, ground cumin, salt, *garam masala* and half the fresh coriander. Mix everything through the onion and tomato base and cook uncovered for 3 minutes. Enjoy the amazing aromas coming from your pan.

Add the drained peas and warm water, give everything a good stir and cook for 2 minutes. Turn the heat down to low and add the grated *paneer*, gently folding it in, then cook for only 1 minute more before removing from the heat – the residual heat from the sauce will finish the cooking process.

Leave to rest uncovered for a few minutes, then garnish with the remaining coriander and serve with *jeera baath* (page 214).

SUKHU KOBI WATTANA cabbage & pea curry

(V, WF, OG, N, HO)

Frozen peas were definitely not around when I was learning to cook in India, but I wish they had been! They are a fantastic time-saver in the kitchen and I love the sweetness they bring to dishes. This is quite a healthy dry curry, and my youngest son, Mayur, enjoys eating it when he is on one of his latest 'get-fit' plans. It may be good for you, but it also has the most incredible balance of flavours. You can use ordinary frozen peas, or even fresh ones, but I think frozen petit pois are the best.

SERVES 4

Masala
3–6 fresh green chillies (ideally Kenyan), trimmed but not de-seeded
3cm root ginger, peeled and roughly chopped
pinch of salt

100ml sunflower oil
2 tsp cumin seeds
1 tsp mustard seeds
¼ tsp asafetida
1 medium cabbage (approx. 585g), cut into 2cm strips
250g frozen petits pois peas, thawed
¼ tsp turmeric
3 tsp ground coriander
1 tsp ground cumin
2 tsp salt
2 handfuls fresh coriander, washed and roughly chopped
75ml boiling water (only if using fresh peas)

Crush the chillies and ginger together with a pinch of salt using a pestle and mortar (or a blender), to make a fine masala paste.

Heat the oil in a thick-based pan for 2 minutes. Add the cumin seeds and swirl through the oil. As soon as they start to froth, add the mustard seeds, swirl through the oil and when they start to pop stir in the asafetida.

Use a wooden or heatproof plastic spoon to stir in the cabbage whilst on a medium heat and cook for 1 minute uncovered, softening the cabbage and infusing it with spices. Now stir in the peas, followed by the masala paste, turmeric, ground coriander, ground cumin, salt and 1 handful of fresh coriander, plus the boiling water (if using fresh peas – I find that frozen peas don't need it). Cover the pan and leave to cook for 7 minutes, gently stirring every so often.

Remove from the heat, sprinkle with the remaining fresh coriander, re-cover and leave to rest for 5 minutes to let the flavours develop. Serve with *makai rotla* (page 202) or, for a more substantial meal, with *baath* (page 213), *shimla mirch* (page 237) and *dhal* (page 228).

SHIMLA MAKAI & pepper & sweetcorn curry
(V, WF, HO)

The reds, yellows and greens really sing out from this dish – it's as much a treat for the eye as it is for the tummy. The bright colours remind me of the food markets in India, where hundreds of different spices are piled high wherever you look. Tinned sweetcorn may not be very authentic, but it's a great cheap and convenient alternative to using fresh corncobs, and a very handy item to keep in your cupboard for mid-week dinner emergencies. Its namesake sweetness complements the earthy flavours from the peppers.

SERVES 4

Masala
4–6 fresh green chillies (ideally Kenyan), trimmed but not de-seeded
3–4 cloves of garlic, soaked and peeled
3cm root ginger, peeled and roughly chopped
pinch of salt

100ml sunflower oil
2 tsp cumin seeds
1 tsp mustard seeds
¼ tsp asafetida
1 medium red pepper, washed and cut in 1cm dice
1 medium green pepper, washed and cut in 1cm dice
1 medium yellow pepper, washed and cut in 1cm dice
1¼ tsp salt
¼ tsp turmeric
2 tsp ground coriander
½ tsp ground cumin
2 handfuls fresh coriander, washed and finely chopped
2 x 300g tins sweetcorn, with juice
2 tsp sesame seeds, toasted

Crush the chillies, garlic and ginger together with a pinch of salt using a pestle and mortar (or a blender), to make a fine masala paste.

Heat the oil in a thick-based pan for 2 minutes. Add the cumin seeds and swirl through the oil. As soon as they start to froth, add the mustard seeds, swirl through the oil and when they start to pop, stir in the asafetida. Now add the diced peppers and stir them through the oil, letting them cook uncovered for 1 minute so that the spices infuse them whilst they soften slightly.

Mix in the masala paste, salt, turmeric, ground coriander, ground cumin and quarter of the fresh coriander. Stir and cook covered for 1 minute. Pour in the sweetcorn straight from the tins, juice and all, and cook covered on a medium heat for 8–9 minutes, stirring halfway through. Take off the heat and leave to rest covered for 10 minutes.

Reheat over a medium heat until piping hot, then sprinkle with the remaining fresh coriander and the sesame seeds. Serve with *masala* chips (page 224) and salad.

RAJMA ◦ classic Punjabi-style kidney bean curry

(V, WF, N, HO)

This is another great recipe, based on a very traditional dish from the Punjab, which I've updated to take advantage of some time-saving ingredients you can pick up easily at the supermarket. Rather than soaking dried beans or peas for hours and then boiling them (as we would have done when I was growing up), you can just use a few tins of kidney beans. You miss out on some of the delicious aromas of the beans cooking away for hours, but with minimal fuss and effort you can produce a really delicious, nourishing meal that is rich in protein.

SERVES 4

Masala
2–4 fresh green chillies (ideally Kenyan), trimmed but not de-seeded
2–4 cloves of garlic, soaked and peeled
4cm root ginger, peeled and roughly chopped
pinch of salt

100ml sunflower oil
1½ tsp cumin seeds
¼ tsp asafetida
1 medium onion, chopped or blended to a smooth texture
1 x 400g tin peeled plum tomatoes, chopped or blended to a smooth texture (NB don't wash the blender yet)
1 tsp turmeric
3 tsp ground coriander
1 tsp ground cumin
2 tsp salt
1 tsp sugar
2 handful fresh coriander, washed and finely chopped
200ml hot water
3 x 400g tins kidney beans in brine, thoroughly rinsed and drained

Crush the chillies, garlic and ginger together with a pinch of salt using a pestle and mortar (or a blender), to make a fine masala paste

Heat the oil in a large thick-based pan for 2 minutes over a medium heat, then add the cumin seeds and swirl through the warm oil. Once they start to froth, stir in the asafetida and add the blended onion – be careful, as the moisture content in the onion is high and it may spit in the oil. Cover and cook until dark brown. This usually takes about 6 minutes but may vary – I check it every couple of minutes, stirring and scraping the onion off the bottom of the pan.

Stir in the blended tomatoes and cook uncovered for 1 minute – just enough time for them to warm up and take a little cumin flavour. Now add the masala paste, turmeric, ground coriander, ground cumin, salt, sugar and half the fresh coriander. Give everything a good stir and leave for 1 minute uncovered to cook together and infuse.

Pour the hot water into the blender and swirl to catch any remaining tomato purée, making sure that nothing is wasted, then pour into the pan. Mix through and bring to a simmer, then cook covered for 2 minutes. Once all the flavours have come together, mix in the kidney beans, cover and cook for 3 minutes. Take off the heat and sprinkle with the remaining chopped coriander. Cover and leave to rest for around 10 minutes to allow the flavours to develop.

Reheat over a medium heat until piping hot and serve with *bathura* (page 208), or – if you're looking for a quicker meal – with *baath* (page 213) or a salad.

CHORA ⟨ black-eyed bean curry
(V, WF, N, HO)

*Pulses are a staple in the Gujarati kitchen: they help to keep up protein levels,
which can sometimes be tricky for vegetarians, and they make you feel good from
the inside out. Mohan is particularly fond of them and so I often make this for him.
A really warming dish, this spicy curry is perfect for a cold night or when you
need some comfort food. If you can't get hold of black-eyed beans, use kidney
beans instead.*

SERVES 4

`Masala`
3–5 fresh green chillies (ideally
  Kenyan), trimmed but not de-seeded
2–4 cloves of garlic, soaked
  and peeled
4cm root ginger, peeled and roughly
  chopped
pinch of salt

100ml sunflower oil
2 tsp cumin seeds
1 tsp mustard seeds
¼ tsp asafetida
1 medium onion, chopped or
  blended to a smooth texture
4 medium vine tomatoes
  (approx. 360g), chopped or
  blended to a coarse pulp
3 tsp ground coriander
1 tsp ground cumin
2 tsp turmeric
2½ tsp salt
1 tsp sugar
2 handfuls fresh coriander,
  washed and finely chopped
300ml boiling water
3 x 400g tins black-eyed beans,
  rinsed and drained

Crush the chillies, garlic and ginger together with a
pinch of salt using a pestle and mortar (or a blender),
to make a fine masala paste.

Heat the oil in a large thick-based pan for 2 minutes
over a medium heat, then add the cumin seeds and
swirl through the warm oil. As soon as they start to
froth, add the mustard seeds and swirl through the
oil once more. When the mustard seeds start to pop,
stir in the asafetida and quickly add the onion –
listen out for the sizzle and enjoy the lovely smell,
but be careful, as the moisture in the onion may
cause the oil to spit.

Cook covered on a medium heat until the onion is
dark brown. This will take approximately 6 minutes;
check every 2 minutes and give it a stir to ensure it
doesn't stick to the bottom and burn.

Add the blended tomatoes, masala paste, ground
coriander, ground cumin, turmeric, salt, sugar and
1 handful of fresh coriander. Stir everything through
and cook uncovered for 1 minute. Now add the
boiling water, turn the heat up and bring to a
simmer. Reduce the heat to medium, add the
black-eyed beans and give everything a good stir
through. Cook half-covered for 8 minutes.

Take off the heat, garnish with the remaining fresh
coriander and leave to rest covered for 10 minutes.

Reheat over a medium heat until piping hot and
serve with *baath* (page 213).

SOYA & WATTANA KEEMA *soya mince & pea curry*

(V, WF, N)

Whenever I make this dish, I think of Ashrafbhai. He is part of the kitchen team at Prashad and he just loves this curry. I am under strict orders that whenever I make it, I have to make double, so that Minal can take some to the restaurant for him to eat. We don't often use meat substitutes but this dish is one of the many examples of the coming together of British and Indian cuisine.

SERVES 4

Masala
6–8 cloves of garlic, soaked
  and peeled
5cm root ginger, peeled and
  roughly chopped
pinch of salt

75ml sunflower oil
3cm cinnamon stick
3 large Indian bay leaves,
  washed
1 tsp mustard seeds
½ tsp asafetida
2 medium onions, cut in 1cm dice
3 medium vine tomatoes, cut in
  1cm dice
1¼ tsp medium red chilli powder
2 tsp *garam masala*
1 tsp turmeric
2 tsp salt
2 tsp ground coriander
½ tsp ground cumin
120g frozen petits pois peas,
  thawed
125ml hot water
100g dried soya mince, soaked in
  1 ltr warm water for 20 minutes
1 handful fresh coriander,
  washed and finely chopped

Crush the garlic and ginger together with a pinch of salt using a pestle and mortar (or a blender), to make a fine masala paste.

Heat the oil in a large thick-based pan for 2 minutes over a medium heat, then add the cinnamon and bay leaves. Swirl them through the warm oil and let the flavours infuse for 30 seconds. Now add the mustard seeds and swirl once more. When the mustard seeds start to pop, stir in the asafetida and onions. Give the onions a really good stir through, making sure the spice-infused oil coats them all, then increase the heat to high and fry for 4 minutes, stirring regularly. Mix in the tomatoes and cook covered for 5 minutes, checking occasionally and giving everything a quick stir.

Add the masala paste, chilli powder, *garam masala*, turmeric, salt, ground coriander and ground cumin and mix them all through – the smells will be amazing by now. Stir in the peas and the hot water. Cover the pan and cook on a medium heat for 4 minutes. Finally, drain the soya and stir in along with the fresh coriander. Take off the heat and leave to rest covered for 10 minutes.

Reheat over a medium heat until piping hot and serve with *palak puri* (page 219) or *tameta pilau* (page 211).

PAV BHAJI ❧ mashed vegetable curry rolls

PANEER TIKKA ❧ griddled pepper & *paneer*

DHAL FRY ❧ spicy lentil curry

MUNG DHAL ❧ green *mung* bean curry

RAGDHA PETHIS ❧ mushy pea soup with potato patties

METHI BHAJI BATAKA ❧ curried fresh fenugreek & potatoes

MUNG VADHU ❧ spiced sprouted *mung* beans

KARELLA NA REVEYA ❧ stuffed bitter melon satay

SUKHU PARVAR BATAKA ❧ pointed gourd and potato curry

UTTAPAM ❧ South Indian mixed vegetable pancakes

RENGHAN BHARTA ❧ smoky mashed aubergine curry

IDLI SAMBAR ❧ steamed dumplings

VEGETABLE KORMA ❧ mild creamy curry

DUM ALOO ❧ bay leaf infused new potato curry

TURAI PATRA ❧ courgette and spinach parcels

BHAGAT MUTHIA ❧ lentil dough ball curry

RAJASTHANI GATTA ❧ Rajasthani dough ball curry

SABZI & PANEER MAKNI ❧ creamy *paneer* curry

Think of these slow suppers a little like you might a Sunday roast or a stew that you can leave bubbling away while you busy yourself with something else. They're not at all difficult, but they are for when you have a bit more time to spend in the kitchen. Some of them involve some simple prep the night before, and there are likely to be a few more stages and processes than the Speedy Suppers recipes in the previous chapter. But they are all just as easy!

Most of the recipes are very traditional dishes I learnt to cook in India – with a few Kaushy additions, of course. We cook quite a few of these dishes in the restaurant, such as the *paneer tikka* and *uttapam* (pages 69 and 85), because the combinations of flavours are unbeatable. I think what brings them all together, though, is that they are great for sharing around the table, making them perfect for larger gatherings and dinner parties. But that doesn't mean you should save them just for this – they are equally good mid-week if you are feeling a bit more energetic and have the time to make them.

When I was first engaged to Mohan, I was introduced to all of his family and, as is the custom, I was asked to cook for them. Of course, I was keen to impress my future in-laws and so made lots of different dishes to share around, Indian-style. As part of that memorable meal, I made *pav bhaji* and a version of *dhal fry* (pages 68 and 71). The colours were so beautiful and it must have gone down well, as my handsome husband agreed to go ahead with the wedding and we're celebrating our forty-seventh anniversary this year!

As you know by now, I think food is all about enjoyment. Take your time with these recipes: making them should be just as much a pleasure as eating them – well, almost. I like to serve up quite small portions at first and then put the rest in big dishes in the middle of the table with a pile of breads and bowls of rice and any other accompaniments alongside. I think this helps keep everyone focussed on the wonderful food, and we can take our time to eat it, savouring each mouthful and helping each other to second portions – rather than just guzzling it down.

PAV BHAJI ‹ mashed vegetable curry rolls

(N)

This dish originated to the south of Gujarat, in the Maharashtra region of India. In Marathi 'pau' means bread or bun, while 'bhaji' means vegetable curry, and it is exactly what the name suggests – veggie curry on a buttered roll! They are a really popular street food and I learnt to cook them when I was about twelve years old. In the restaurant, Minal serves these using fresh garlic naan breads instead of the rolls, renaming the dish naan bhaji.

SERVES 4

12 finger buns, sliced and buttered

Masala
6–8 fresh green chillies (ideally Kenyan), trimmed but not de-seeded
2–4 cloves of garlic, soaked and peeled
4cm root ginger, peeled and roughly chopped
pinch of salt

100ml sunflower oil
2 tsp cumin seeds
3 medium red-skinned (or other waxy) potatoes, peeled and cut in 1½cm dice
1 large carrot, peeled and cut in 1½cm dice
100g frozen petits pois peas, thawed
380g cauliflower, finely chopped
100g salted butter, cut in 1cm cubes
1½ tsp salt
2 handfuls fresh coriander, washed and finely chopped
325ml warm water
5 tsp *pav bhaji masala* powder
3 vine tomatoes, blended to a smooth pulp
1 tsp medium red chilli powder

To finish
1 medium red onion, cut in ½cm dice
2 medium vine tomatoes, cut in ½cm dice
1 fresh lemon, quartered

Crush the chillies, garlic and ginger together with a pinch of salt using a pestle and mortar (or a blender), to make a fine masala paste.

Heat the oil in a large thick-based frying pan on a medium heat for 2 minutes, then add the cumin seeds. Swirl them in the warm oil and when they start to froth, mix in the potatoes and carrot, making sure the spice-infused oil coats the vegetables. Cook for 30 seconds, then stir in the peas and cauliflower. Cook uncovered for 1 minute, then gently stir through the butter cubes. Once the butter has melted, cover and cook for 14 minutes, stirring every couple of minutes to ensure nothing is sticking to the pan. Add the masala paste, salt and 1 handful of fresh coriander, stir, re-cover and cook for 4 minutes, stirring halfway through.

Now take the pan off the heat and use a potato masher to mash the hot vegetables until you have a chunky texture. You are essentially squeezing the spices into the veg, so do this slowly and gently, making sure you don't lose any over the edge of pan.

Place back on a medium heat, gently stir in the warm water and cook uncovered for 2 minutes. Now stir in the *pav bhaji masala* powder, bring to a simmer and cook for 1 minute to allow it to work its magic. Stir in the blended tomatoes, cover and cook for 8 minutes, stirring every 2 minutes. Mix in the chilli powder, re-cover and cook for a further 5 minutes, after which take the pan off the heat and leave to rest covered for 10 minutes.

Gently toast the buttered finger buns on both sides in a griddle or frying pan. Serve the buns covered generously with the curry. Garnish with the red onion, vine tomato and remaining coriander, and a little squeeze of lemon.

PANEER TIKKA <small>&</small> griddled pepper & *paneer*

(WF, N, HO)

There is a bit of a Mediterranean feel to this dish, but it uses very traditional Gujarati ingredients. The cheese is griddled so it takes on a bit of sweetness where it has caramelised to perfection. You could very easily eat it with just some simply cooked rice, but I recommend taking a bit of time to make tameta pilau *(page 211),* chana chaat patti *(page 244) and maybe even some crunchy* kakra bhajia *(page 221) to eat alongside.*

SERVES 4

Masala
4–6 fresh green chillies (ideally Kenyan), trimmed but not de-seeded
4–6 cloves of garlic, soaked and peeled
3cm root ginger, peeled and roughly chopped
pinch of salt

2 tsp salt
½ tsp ground black pepper
juice of 1 lime
1 tsp turmeric
2 tsp ground coriander
½ tsp ground cumin
1½ tsp *garam masala*
30g gram (chickpea) flour, sieved
260g *paneer* cheese, cut in 3cm dice
8 medium chestnut mushrooms, halved
1½ red or green peppers, cut in 12 pieces
20ml sunflower oil
1 handful fresh coriander, washed and finely chopped

Crush the chillies, garlic and ginger together with a pinch of salt using a pestle and mortar (or a blender), to make a fine masala paste.

Mix the masala paste, salt, pepper, lime juice, turmeric, ground coriander, ground cumin, *garam masala* and gram flour in a large bowl. Rub the marinade you have created between your fingers and thumbs, working the flavours together. Let it rest for a few minutes.

Place the *paneer* pieces in the marinade and gently mix through. Repeat with the mushrooms and then the peppers, making sure everything gets a good coating of the marinade. Leave to infuse for 1 hour.

Heat a griddle pan (or a large frying pan) on medium heat for 3 minutes. Pour in the oil and gently lay the vegetables and *paneer* in the pan. Fry for 2 minutes on each side or until cooked through.

When everything is golden brown and soft, serve piping hot, garnished with the fresh coriander, on a bed of *tameta pilau* (page 211) with *chana chaat patti* (page 244) and/or *kakra bhajia* (page 221).

DHAL FRY ⸱ spicy lentil curry

(WF, N, HO)

This is the original working man's dinner. I remember my grandmother making enormous pots of dhal *in the afternoon, ready to ladle spoonfuls of it into the bowls of the hungry farmers at the end of the day. Traditionally, it is made using dried pigeon beans, but when we first moved to the UK, we couldn't source them very easily. Yellow lentils make a very good substitute and they don't take as long to cook either.*

SERVES 4

Masala
3–5 fresh green chillies (ideally Kenyan), trimmed but not de-seeded
2–3cm root ginger, peeled and roughly chopped
pinch of salt

100g *tuvar dhal* (dried pigeon peas / yellow lentils)
100g *masoor dhal* (red split lentils)
100g *mung dhal* (yellow split mung beans)
1.1 ltr boiling water
3 tsp sunflower oil, plus 100ml
2 tsp cumin seeds
3–4 dried red chillies
2cm cinnamon stick
¼ tsp asafetida
1 medium onion, cut in 1cm dice
4 cloves garlic, peeled and cut in very thin slices
2¼ tsp salt
1½ tsp turmeric
3 tsp ground coriander
½ tsp ground cumin
2 handfuls fresh coriander, washed and finely chopped
20g salted butter

Crush the chillies and ginger together with a pinch of salt using a pestle and mortar (or a blender), to make a fine masala paste.

Wash the *tuvar dhal* in hot water in a large pan and drain in a sieve. Repeat until the drained water is no longer cloudy. Add the other two *dhals* to the pan and wash again, this time with cold water, squeezing the pulses through your fingers. Drain and repeat until the drained water is almost clear.

Place the drained pulses back in the empty pan along with 900ml of the boiling water and 3 teaspoons of sunflower oil (this helps prevent the water from boiling over). Place on full heat and bring to a simmer, then three-quarters cover the pan and cook for 15 minutes on a medium heat. Add the remaining 200ml of boiling water, three-quarters cover the pan again and simmer for a further 5 minutes. Check the *dhals* are cooked (they should be easy to squash between your finger and thumb with no hard centres) then remove from the heat.

Heat the 100ml of sunflower oil in a pan on a medium heat for 1½ minutes. Add the cumin seeds and swirl through the oil. Break the dried chillies in half and swirl them through the oil, then add the cinnamon stick and asafetida. Let the oil infuse for 30 seconds, then stir in the onion. Cook for 6 minutes, stirring regularly, then add the garlic and cook for a further 1½ minutes. Add the masala paste, salt, turmeric, ground coriander, ground

CONTINUED OVERLEAF

cumin and a handful of fresh coriander, mix through and cook for 2 minutes.

Transfer the spiced onion mixture to the *dhal* pan and cook uncovered on a medium heat for 2 minutes. Stir in the butter until it melts, then remove the pan from the heat and leave to rest covered for 10 minutes.

Reheat over a medium heat until piping hot, garnish with the remaining fresh coriander and serve with *makai rotla* (page 202) and/or *barela marcha* (page 243).

MUNG DHAL ⟨ green *mung* bean curry

(V, WF, OG, N, HO)

I predict that this mung dhal *will be an instant family favourite. There is a lovely slight sweetness coming from the jaggery and the whole green* mung *beans have a light, almost melt-in-the-mouth texture. Traditionally, it is eaten cold with* rotli *for an authentic Indian breakfast, but it also makes a satisfying, warming evening meal with plenty of crusty bread. I always make extra so that the leftovers can thicken up overnight, as my sons can't resist it straight from the fridge! Whether hot or cold, I guarantee it'll be a hit.*

SERVES 4

250g whole dried green *mung* beans, washed three times and drained

2 ltr boiling water

1 x 400g tin peeled plum tomatoes, chopped or blended to a smooth texture

2 handfuls fresh coriander, washed and finely chopped

3cm fresh ginger, peeled and pulped

3 tsp salt

2 tsp turmeric

2 tsp medium red chilli powder

2 tsp ground coriander

½ tsp ground cumin

25g *jaggery*, cut into thin flakes (or demerara / soft brown sugar)

75ml sunflower oil

4 dried red chillies

1 tsp fenugreek seeds

2 tsp mustard seeds

¼ tsp asafetida

1 lemon, quartered

Put the *mung* beans in a large deep pan with 1 litre of boiling water. Bring to the boil on high heat and watch that it does not boil over. Boil until most of the water has cooked off (approximately 10 minutes), then add a further 700ml of boiling water and cook for 12 minutes. Finally add the remaining 300ml of water and boil for 5 minutes, until the *mung* beans are cooked.

Take off the heat and stir in the tomatoes, 1 handful of fresh coriander, ginger, salt, turmeric, chilli powder, ground coriander, ground cumin and *jaggery* and leave to rest covered until you have finished infusing the oil.

In a separate pan, heat the oil for 1 minute on a medium heat. Break the dried chillies in half and add to the pan with the fenugreek seeds and mustard seeds. When the mustard seeds start to pop, add the asafetida and stir for 30 seconds. Take off the heat and leave to infuse for 1 minute.

Carefully take a small ladleful of the *mung* mixture and gently pour it into the hot oil. Let it sizzle and smell like heaven. Add a second ladleful of *mung* to the oil, then pour the spicy oil–*mung* mix into the large pan containing the remaining *mung* and stir through. Place the *mung* pan on a medium heat and cook uncovered for 7 minutes, stirring occasionally. Take off the heat and leave to rest covered for 10 minutes.

Reheat over a medium heat until piping hot, then sprinkle with the remaining fresh coriander, a squeeze of fresh lemon and serve with *rotli* (page 206), *baath* (page 213) and *khudi* (page 226).

RAGDHA PETHIS ❁ mushy pea soup with potato patties

(V, WF, N, HO)

Now, I'm going to let you into a little secret here: my family loves this chaat-style dish so much that they've insisted we don't serve it at the restaurant and keep it solely to enjoy at home. It's the family chaat jewel! There may be lots of ingredients here, and it does take a while, but believe me it's worth it. You need to soak the peas for at least eight hours before you start cooking, so this is one to plan ahead for – make it a weekly treat that all the family will look forward to. Use fresh lemon juice in the patties if you prefer, but I like the more concentrated flavour you get from bottled juice.

SERVES 4

Masala for ragdha – crush together using a pestle and mortar (or a blender) to make a fine paste

1–2 fresh green chillies (ideally Kenyan), trimmed but not de-seeded

1–2 cloves of garlic, soaked and peeled

2cm root ginger, peeled and roughly chopped

pinch of salt

Ragdha

300g dried green peas, soaked in water for at least 8 hours, then drained

2.9 ltr boiling water

75ml sunflower oil

2 tsp cumin seeds

½ tsp asafetida

2 tsp ground coriander

2 tsp salt

Masala for patties – crush together using a pestle and mortar (or a blender) to make a fine paste

2–4 fresh green chillies (ideally Kenyan), trimmed but not de-seeded

2–4 cloves of garlic, soaked and peeled

pinch of salt

Put the peas and the boiling water in a pressure cooker with an 80g lid. Cook on a medium heat until it has whistled twice (this should take roughly 10 minutes). Place the pressure cooker under cold running water to help release the steam and enable you to open it easily.

If you don't have a pressure cooker, you can put the peas and 1 litre of boiling water in a large pan and three-quarters cover with the lid, being careful not to let the lid slip fully onto the pan as the water will boil over onto the hob. Simmer over a full heat for about 20 minutes, then add another litre of boiling water, three-quarters cover again and simmer on full heat for 25 minutes. Add the remaining 900ml of boiling water and simmer three-quarters covered for 30–35 minutes, until the mixture has thickened and about half the peas have split. Take off the heat.

Heat the oil and cumin seeds in a small pan over a medium heat. When the seeds start to darken, stir in the asafetida and ground coriander and cook for 1 minute. Pour the spiced oil into the pressure cooker or soup pan with the peas, add the salt and *ragdha* masala paste and mix well. Simmer over a medium heat for 3 minutes, then set aside until needed.

Boil the potatoes in their skins for 40 minutes or so until a knife tip will slide in easily. (It is important that you boil the potatoes in their skins and then peel

Patties
3 medium red-skinned (or other
  waxy) potatoes
3 tsp cornflour, sieved
1½ tsp salt
1 handful fresh coriander, washed
  and finely chopped
1 tsp sugar
4 tbsp bottled or fresh lemon juice
2 slices white bread
75ml sunflower oil for frying

To serve
8 tbsp *imli* chutney (page 241)
1 medium red onion, finely chopped
150g *sev* (Indian chickpea vermicelli)
2–4 green chillies (ideally Ghanaian),
  trimmed and finely chopped in rings
1 handful fresh coriander, washed
  and finely chopped

them after cooking, as this ensures that they do not absorb too much water and keeps all their flavour.) Soak them in cold water for a minute, then peel and mash. Mix the mashed potato, cornflour, salt, coriander, patties masala paste, sugar and lemon juice in a large bowl. Dip the bread into cold water to soak, then squeeze out all the water and crumble into the mashed potato mix. Mix well to combine.

Divide the mixture into 12 and use the palm of your hand to make each one into a flat disc approximately 6cm in diameter and 1½cm thick. Place these patties on a tray or large plate.

Heat the oil in a large non-stick frying pan on a low heat. Put five or six patties in the pan, turn up the heat slightly and cook for 5 minutes on each side until golden brown and crispy. Repeat with the remaining patties until they have all been fried. While the patties are frying, reheat the *ragdha* on a medium heat until gently bubbling.

Place 3 patties in each bowl, pour a couple of ladles of *ragdha* around them, drizzle with a couple of tablespoons of *imli* chutney, then sprinkle with chopped onion and a handful of *sev*. Add chilli rings to taste and garnish with fresh coriander.

Tuck in while it's steaming hot, then sit back and enjoy the warm, sleepy feeling that follows a really filling meal. In fact, eating *ragdha pethis* makes us so sleepy that it's a great way to ensure that we all get an early night.

METHI BHAJI BATAKA ❧ curried fresh fenugreek & potatoes

(V, WF, N, HO)

In the garden in India, we grew masses of fresh herbs and spices that we'd pick fresh to use every day or dry out for during the monsoon season. The Yorkshire climate doesn't lend itself as well to most of those sun-loving chillies and spices, but fenugreek doesn't seem to mind the cold. Picking it from the pots in our garden here, then cooking with it straight away in the kitchen, reminds me of my grandmother.

SERVES 4

2 bunches (approx. 250g) fresh
  fenugreek leaves
100ml sunflower oil
2 tsp fenugreek seeds
¼ tsp asafetida
8 cloves of garlic, soaked,
  peeled and sliced into 2mm discs
3 medium red-skinned (or other
  waxy) potatoes, peeled and cut in
  2cm dice
2 medium vine tomatoes,
  washed and cut in 2cm dice,
  keeping all the juices
2½ tsp salt
2 tsp medium red chilli powder
1½ tsp turmeric
2½ tsp ground coriander
½ tsp ground cumin

Rinse and trim the fresh fenugreek leaves, then cut in 1cm-wide strips. Leave uncovered at room temperature overnight to dry. Cutting the fenugreek leaves in advance helps them to dry out so that they can absorb more flavour when cooking.

Heat the oil in a large thick frying pan for 2 minutes over a medium heat before adding the fenugreek seeds, asafetida and garlic. Gently let them brown for 30 seconds, infusing the oil. Stir in the potatoes and cook covered on a medium heat for 10 minutes, stirring and turning them every couple of minutes.

Stir in the tomatoes, salt, chilli powder, turmeric, ground coriander and ground cumin. Add the fresh fenugreek leaves, gently stir through and cook covered for 7 minutes, stirring occasionally as the fenugreek wilts and cooks.

Serve piping hot with *baath* (page 213) and *khudi* (page 226).

MUNG VADHU ✿ spiced sprouted *mung* beans

(V, WF, N, HO)

All the men in our family have inherited what we consider a very honourable family trait: the propensity to grow a bit of a belly from time to time. Whenever they are watching what they eat, they really enjoy mung vadhu. *It's very filling but also low in fat. You'll need to make a start on this two days before you want to eat it, but it's well worth the effort. By sprouting the beans you increase their nutritional value, while at the same time enabling them to absorb more flavour during cooking.*

SERVES 4

350g whole dried green *mung* beans
1 ltr lukewarm water

Masala
2–5 fresh green chillies (ideally Kenyan), trimmed but not de-seeded
4cm root ginger, peeled and roughly chopped
pinch of salt

100ml sunflower oil
2 tsp mustard seeds
½ tsp asafetida
1 tsp turmeric
3 tsp ground coriander
½ tsp ground cumin
2½ tsp salt
½ tsp sugar
500ml boiling water
1 handful fresh coriander, washed and finely chopped

Soak the *mung* beans in the lukewarm water in a large, lidded pan. Do not run your hands through them because they won't sprout as well. Cover the pan and set in a warm place for 16 hours (I leave them overnight next to a radiator). The next day, drain the beans and gently wash them in warm water. Now wrap them in a muslin cloth and tie it tightly. Place the bundle back in the pan, re-cover and leave overnight in the same place. The following day, remove the *mung* beans from the cloth, check through them and throw out all the unsprouted ones (there will usually only be one or two). Rinse the sprouted *mung* with cold water and leave to drain.

Crush the chillies and ginger together with a pinch of salt using a pestle and mortar (or a blender), to make a fine masala paste.

Heat the oil in a large thick-based pan on a medium heat for about 2 minutes. Add the mustard seeds, swirl them in the oil and when they start to pop, add the asafetida and swirl again. Add the *mung* beans, masala paste, turmeric, ground coriander, ground cumin, salt and sugar, pour in the boiling water and gently stir to combine.

Cover and cook covered for about 15 minutes, gently stirring every 5 minutes. Check the beans are cooked by squeezing one between finger and thumb – careful, as it will be hot – it should be soft. Now add half the fresh coriander, stir and leave to rest covered for 10 minutes.

When you are ready to eat, reheat over a low heat until piping hot and garnish with the remaining fresh coriander. Serve with a bowl of *khudi* (page 226) and a mixed salad.

KARELLA NA REVEYA ⟨ stuffed bitter melon satay
(V, WF, HO)

Gujaratis are well known for having a bit of a sweet tooth, and the jaggery in this recipe really helps to balance the flavours from the bitter melon to produce a well-rounded dish. Bitter melons (also known as bitter gourds) can vary in taste depending on how ripe they are – the rule of thumb is that the yellower the skin, the more bitter they will be, so if you want a milder flavour, go for the greenest ones you can find. Give the dish a taste just before you leave it to rest to see whether it needs a little extra jaggery.

SERVES 4

Masala

3–5 fresh green chillies (ideally Kenyan), trimmed but not de-seeded

4cm root ginger, peeled and roughly chopped

pinch of salt

200g red-skinned (unroasted, unsalted) peanuts, finely chopped or blended

50g *jaggery*, cut in thin flakes (or demerara / soft brown sugar), plus more to taste (if needed)

3 tsp ground coriander

1 tsp ground cumin

2 tsp turmeric

2¼ tsp salt

1 tsp cumin seeds

½ tsp asafetida

1 large tomato, finely chopped or blended

5 medium bitter melons (approx. 500g), washed

150ml sunflower oil

2 medium red-skinned (or other waxy) potatoes, peeled and cut in 1cm dice

2½ handfuls fresh coriander, washed and finely chopped

40ml lukewarm water

Crush the chillies and ginger together with a pinch of salt using a pestle and mortar (or a blender), to make a fine masala paste.

Mix together the peanuts, *jaggery*, masala paste, ground coriander, ground cumin, turmeric, salt, cumin seeds, asafetida and tomato in a large bowl using your hands, working the spices through with your fingertips. Leave to rest for a few minutes to allow the spices to infuse.

Cut each bitter melon into 3 equal chunks (so you have two ends and a middle section). Slice lengthways down one side of each chunk, cutting about halfway into it. Gently prise open so that you can remove all the pulp from the middle, but try to avoid splitting the chunk in half, as you want to be able to fill it with the nutty marinade.

Heat the oil in a large lidded frying pan on a medium heat. Add the bitter melon and potatoes and cook covered for 10 minutes. Turn the pieces and cook for a further 5 minutes. Take the bitter melon and potatoes out of the pan one by one, draining the infused oil back into the pan as you go, and place on a plate.

Pour the oil into the spice and tomato marinade you made earlier and add 2 handfuls of fresh coriander. Leave to stand for a few minutes to let the oil cool, then mix through.

Gently fill the bitter melons with the marinade. Lay each piece on its side in the frying pan. Mix the potatoes with the remaining marinade, then place with the melons in the frying pan. Put the pan on a low heat. Pour the lukewarm water into the marinade bowl and use to wash all the remaining marinade into the frying pan, making sure that nothing is wasted. Cook covered for 20 minutes, gently turning the melons and potatoes halfway through.

Taste a piece of the cooked bitter melon to check whether the dish needs more sweetness to balance the flavours. If it does, sprinkle with some additional *jaggery* flakes – they will melt into the sauce while it rests. Take off the heat and leave to rest uncovered for 10 minutes, then garnish with the remaining fresh coriander.

Serve hot with fresh *rotli* (page 206), *tameta pilau* (page 211) and *khudi* (page 226).

SUKHU PARVAR BATAKA ⟨ pointed gourd and potato curry

(V, WF, OG, N, HO)

Indian village life is all about eating with the seasons and parvar *starts to appear in the markets there in February. When I was little, I remember thinking when we ate the first* parvar *of the year that it was nearly time for Holi – the Hindu festival of colour, to mark the beginning of spring. We celebrate it here too: the team from the restaurant get dressed up in plain white kufnis and throw colourful paints at each other for this happy occasion.*

SERVES 4

Masala
4–6 fresh green chillies (ideally Kenyan), trimmed but not de-seeded
3cm root ginger, peeled and roughly chopped
pinch of salt

500g pointed gourd (about 12–15 gourds)
2 medium red-skinned (or other waxy) potatoes
100ml sunflower oil
2 tsp mustard seeds
¼ tsp asafetida
2 tsp salt
1 tsp turmeric
3 tsp ground coriander
1 tsp ground cumin
1½ tsp sugar
1 handful fresh coriander, washed and finely chopped

Crush the chillies and ginger together with a pinch of salt using a pestle and mortar (or a blender), to make a fine masala paste.

Wash the gourds, cut off the top and tail, slice in half, scoop out any black seeds, and cut in thin (3–5mm) slices lengthways. Peel the potatoes and cut into similar-sized strips.

Heat the oil in a large thick-based frying pan on a medium heat for about 2 minutes. Add the mustard seeds, and when they start to pop, use a wooden or heatproof plastic spoon to stir in the asafetida and potato strips, ensuring that the potatoes are well-coated in oil. Increase the heat to high and fry for 2 minutes, then stir in the gourd slices and return the heat to medium.

Gently stir in the salt and turmeric, cover and leave to cook for 3 minutes. Add the masala paste, ground coriander, ground cumin, sugar and half the fresh coriander and stir gently, being careful not to break the delicate gourds. Cover and leave to cook for 8 minutes, stirring every 2 minutes and scraping up any goodness sticking to the bottom of the pan. Add the remaining fresh coriander, stir through, then remove the pan from the heat and leave to rest, covered, for about 5 minutes to allow the flavours to infuse.

Reheat over a low heat until piping hot, and serve with *rotli* (page 206), *dhal* (page 228) and *baath* (page 213).

UTTAPAM ~ South Indian mixed vegetable pancakes

(WF, N, HO)

When I make these pancakes, I always want to add more and different vegetables – they just taste so good. Experiment with your favourite veggies – but make sure you cut them to roughly the same size, so they cook through evenly. Don't worry if, when you're making the batter, it sticks to the vegetables at first; just keep stirring and eventually everything will come together. I sometimes make up and cook a quarter of the batter at a time, so it is as airy as possible when it goes into the pan. Serve with sambar *(page 230) and* kopru coconut chutney *(page 235).*

SERVES 4

Masala
8 fresh green chillies (ideally
  Kenyan), trimmed but not de-seeded
4 cloves of garlic, soaked and peeled
pinch of salt

1 medium red pepper, washed and
  cut in ½cm dice
1 medium yellow pepper, washed and
  cut in ½cm dice
1 medium green pepper, washed and
  cut in ½cm dice
2 medium red onions, peeled and
  cut in ½cm dice
2 medium vine tomatoes, washed
  and cut in ½cm dice, no juice
2 handfuls fresh coriander,
  washed and finely chopped
320g *idli* flour, sieved
200ml warm water
160ml sunflower oil for frying

Crush the chillies and garlic together with a pinch of salt using a pestle and mortar (or a blender), to make a fine masala paste.

Put a quarter of the vegetables and a quarter of the fresh coriander in a large bowl with a quarter of the flour and a quarter of the masala paste. Mix together using your hands, making sure you persevere to work all the flour through. Add 50ml of water and mix again, incorporating as much air as you can and gently folding the vegetables through the batter.

Heat 10ml of sunflower oil in a small, deep frying pan on a medium heat for 1 minute. Put the *uttapam* batter in the pan and gently spread it to the edges. Cover and cook for 6 minutes, then gently ease it off the sides and shake the pan to loosen the bottom. Flip, toss or use a spatula to turn it over, as you would a traditional pancake or omelette, then drizzle 30ml of oil around the edge. Cover and cook for 5 minutes.

Remove from the pan, cut into quarters (so that everyone can have some) and serve with *sambar* (page 230) and *kopru* chutney (page 235). Repeat the process with the remaining ingredients to make another three delicious *uttapam* pancakes.

RENGHAN BHARTA ⟨ Smoky mashed aubergine curry

(V, WF, N, HO)

*Aubergines are great if you follow a vegetable-based diet, as they are very filling.
I was actually first inspired to make this amazing dish, which is very popular in
Maharasthra and Pakistan, after we saw a contestant on a reality-TV show in India
cook it. Like all aubergine dishes, it is now extremely popular in the Patel household.
It is a particularly fun one for aspiring chefs because you get to burn the aubergine
over a naked flame, which gives it a fantastic smoky barbecue taste.*

SERVES 4

Masala
3–4 cloves of garlic, soaked and
  peeled
4cm root ginger, peeled and
  roughly chopped
pinch of salt

1 large aubergine (approx. 480g)
enough sunflower oil to coat the
  aubergine, plus 65ml
3cm cinnamon stick
1 tsp cumin seeds
¼ tsp asafetida
1½ medium onions, cut in
  ½cm dice
3 large vine tomatoes, cut in
  1cm dice
1¾ tsp ground coriander
¼ tsp ground cumin
1½ tsp medium red chilli powder
1 tsp turmeric
2 tsp salt
1 tsp dried fenugreek leaves
2 tsp *garam masala*
100ml warm water
1 handful fresh coriander,
  washed and finely chopped

Crush the garlic and ginger with a pinch of salt using a pestle and mortar (or blender), to make a fine masala paste.

Holding the aubergine by the stem, coat with oil and lay it directly over a medium-high flame. Leave on the naked flame and turn regularly. Continue to do this for 4–5 minutes until the aubergine starts to become floppy and the skin starts to burn and smoke. Reduce the heat to low and (using two forks) continue scorching it for a further 3–4 minutes. The smoke will infuse the aubergine.

Gently dunk the aubergine in cold water and, whilst in the water, peel the skin off. It's OK if you leave a few bits but most must be peeled off. Put the peeled aubergine in a bowl and use a potato masher to mash the flesh – you want a chunky texture, not a smooth paste.

Heat the 65ml of sunflower oil in a pan on a medium heat for 1 minute. Add the cinnamon and let the oil infuse for 10–15 seconds before adding the cumin seeds. Swirl the seeds through the oil and let them infuse for 10–15 seconds, then swirl in the asafetida and add the onions. Cook on a high heat for 3–4 minutes until the onions start to brown. Add the tomatoes and cook covered for 4 minutes, stirring occasionally. Now add the masala paste, ground coriander, ground cumin, chilli powder, turmeric, salt, dried fenugreek leaves and *garam masala*. Give it all a good, gentle mix. Stir in the warm water and cook covered for 3 minutes. Finally, gently stir in the aubergines, cover and cook on a medium heat for 7 minutes. Take off the heat and leave to rest uncovered for 10 minutes.

Reheat over a medium heat until piping hot, then sprinkle with the fresh coriander and serve with *makai rotla* (page 202) and *jeera baath* (page 214).

IDLI SAMBAR ∝ steamed dumplings

(WF, N, HO)

The weekends are very busy, but Monday (when the restaurant is closed) is Bobby and Minal's day off. We like to enjoy a really relaxed family meal together and we'll often have these lovely steamed dumplings. The sambar *(page 230) takes a little time to cook, so put the radio on in the kitchen and just enjoy the process. I usually make extra, as there's always someone who wants a third or fourth helping! You will need an egg poacher or egg-poaching moulds (or an* idli *poacher, obviously) to cook the dumplings.*

SERVES 4

240g *idli* flour, sieved
400ml cold water
sunflower oil, to line
1 batch *sambar* (page 230)
about 4 tbsp *kopru* chutney
  (page 235), or more to taste
1 handful fresh coriander,
  washed and finely chopped

In a small bowl, mix 60g of the *idli* flour and 50ml cold water together using your hands, making sure the flour doesn't all clump together. Add another 50ml water and use your hands to beat the mixture gently to create a light, airy batter. Don't beat it too much or it will start to lose the airiness – we want the *idlis* to be good and fluffy.

Using a brush, line the egg poacher or poached egg moulds with a little oil. I use a third of the batter to make 4 *idli* at a time, but you can make larger or smaller batches depending on the size of your egg poacher / number of poaching moulds. Place in a pan of boiling water and cook covered for 9 minutes. Scoop the cooked *idli* out and repeat until all the batter has been poached (you should have 12 *idli* in total).

Whilst the second batch is cooking, place 2 *idlis* in a large shallow bowl, pour *sambar* around the *idli* and spoon a thick dollop of *kopru* chutney on top. Garnish with the fresh coriander and enjoy. Keeping serving the *idli* 2 at a time to whoever makes it to the front of the queue.

VEGETABLE KORMA ⟨ mild creamy curry

(WF)

Unlike the korma served in most British restaurants, a traditional korma is not actually creamy but as an example of how cultures often combine brilliantly, I have used a splash of cream in this version, to soften the heat of the spices a little. It's a good dish to make for anyone who is a little nervous about eating anything too fiery.

SERVES 6

3 medium carrots, peeled and cut
  in 1cm dice
180g cauliflower, cut into 3cm
  florets
100g French beans, topped and
  tailed and cut in half
4 medium onions, cut in 2cm dice
30ml water (if needed)
75ml sunflower oil
2 Indian bay leaves, washed
3cm cinnamon stick
½ tsp asafetida
2 vine tomatoes, cut in 1cm dice
50g plain live set yoghurt
½ tsp turmeric
2 tsp ground coriander
½ tsp ground cumin
½ tsp *garam masala*
2½ tsp salt
300ml warm water
2cm root ginger, peeled and finely
  chopped into strips
2 fresh green chillies with seeds
  (ideally Kenyan)
2 tsp sugar
6 tsp double cream
180g frozen petits pois peas, thawed
1 handful fresh coriander,
  washed and finely chopped
15 cashew nuts, toasted and coarsely
  crushed

Bring a large pan of water to the boil. Add the carrots and simmer on a medium heat for 4 minutes, then add the cauliflower and French beans and cook for a further 4 minutes. Scoop the vegetables out of the water using a slotted spoon, place in a bowl and set aside.

Put the onions in the boiling water and cook for 5 minutes. Drain the onions, then blend to a fine pulp using either a hand-held blender or a food processor. Depending on the moisture in the onions, you may want to add 30ml of water to enable them to blend properly.

Heat the oil in a thick-based frying pan for 1 minute. Add the bay leaves and cinnamon stick and swirl through the oil for 30 seconds. Swirl in the asafetida, then take the pan off the heat. Carefully add the blended onions at arm's length – they will spit in the hot oil – then cook uncovered on a high heat for 5 minutes, stirring regularly so they don't stick.

Add the chopped tomatoes and cook covered for 3 minutes. Mix in the yoghurt and add the turmeric, ground coriander, ground cumin, *garam masala* and salt. Stir in the warm water to help infuse these flavours into the onions, then cover and cook for 3 minutes. By now, the bay leaves and other flavours will have softly come through. Add the ginger and chillies, cover and cook for 2 minutes. Mix in the sugar and cream, reduce the heat to low and gently stir in the drained vegetables and the peas. Cook uncovered for 3 minutes. Take off the heat and leave to rest covered for 10 minutes.

Reheat over a medium heat until piping hot and garnish with the fresh coriander and toasted cashew nuts. Serve with *rotli* (page 206), to mop up all the sauce.

DUM ALOO · bay leaf infused new potato curry

(V, WF, N, HO)

I was only fifteen when I moved to the UK and it was hard being away from my family and everything that I knew, although I never complained, as it was such an amazing opportunity. Cooking the meals I had learned in India gave me comfort and reassurance. When my daughter-in-law, Minal, first came to live with us, she cooked this dish for the whole family. It is quite a different spice mix from the one we were used to, but it is now a regular in the Patel kitchen.

SERVES 4

Masala

4–6 cloves of garlic, soaked and peeled
4cm root ginger, peeled and roughly chopped
pinch of salt

450g baby new potatoes
sunflower oil for deep-frying, plus 75ml
2cm cinnamon stick
2 Indian bay leaves, washed
1 tsp cumin seeds
¼ tsp asafetida
1 medium onion, peeled and cut in 1cm dice
½ tsp medium red chilli powder
1 tsp turmeric
2 tsp salt
1 tsp *garam masala*
2 tsp ground coriander
¼ tsp ground cumin
4 large vine tomatoes, blended to a smooth pulp
1 handful fresh coriander, washed and finely chopped

Crush the garlic and ginger together with a pinch of salt using a pestle and mortar (or a blender), to make a fine masala paste.

Boil the potatoes in their skins for 35 minutes, then soak in cold water and peel. Cut into roughly 3cm cubes.

Heat the frying oil – about 10cm deep – in a large pan over a high heat (or in a deep fat fryer) and when you think it is hot enough, test the temperature by dropping a potato cube into the oil; the potato should quickly spring back up to float on the surface. Reduce the heat to medium and fry the potatoes for 1–2 minutes until they have a crisp golden coating. Carefully remove them from the oil with a slotted spoon and place on absorbent kitchen towel.

Heat the 75ml of oil in a large thick-based frying pan on a medium heat for 2 minutes. Add the cinnamon and swirl into the oil, infuse for 1 minute and add the bay leaves, cumin seeds and asafetida. Swirl the spices through the oil before adding the onion and turning to full heat. Cook uncovered for 5 minutes.

Add the masala paste, chilli powder, turmeric, salt, *garam masala*, ground coriander and ground cumin. Mix everything through and allow the flavours to combine for 30 seconds. Then stir in the blended tomatoes, bring to a simmer, cover and cook for 8–9 minutes. Finally, stir in the potatoes and cook covered on a medium heat for 4 minutes. Leave to rest covered for at least 10 minutes.

Reheat on a medium heat until piping hot, sprinkle with the fresh coriander and serve with *rotli* (page 206) and *tuvar dhal kichdi* (page 217).

TURAI PATRA ⚮ courgette and spinach parcels

(WF, HO)

In our garden in India we grew many types of squashes in all different colours and shapes. As children, during monsoon season, we would go and check on them before bed when they would be about 10cm wide, but by morning they had often grown up to 25cm wide, from soaking up all the rainwater! We'd rush out and pick them and then make this curry. If you can't find large-leaf spinach, use chard or other big leafy greens instead; regular spinach leaves won't work, as they are too small.

SERVES 4

SPINACH PARCELS

32 large spinach leaves,
  approx. 14cm x 11cm, washed

*Masala – crush together using
a pestle and mortar (or a blender)
to make a fine paste*
2–3 fresh green chillies (ideally
  Kenyan), trimmed but not
  de-seeded
2–3 cloves of garlic, soaked and
  peeled
2cm root ginger, peeled and
  roughly chopped
pinch of salt

Paste
100g gram (chickpea) flour, sieved
40g sorghum flour, sieved
1 tsp salt
42g *jaggery*, finely chopped
  (or demerara / soft brown sugar)
4 tsp bottled or fresh lemon juice
1 tsp carom seeds
pinch of turmeric
2 tsp ground coriander
½ tsp ground cumin

Place the washed spinach leaves vein-side up on a chopping board and using a small knife chop off the root as close to the leaf as possible. Roll over the main vein with a rolling pin, squashing it into the leaf.

Sieve the flours into a medium bowl. Add the masala paste, salt, *jaggery*, lemon juice, carom seeds, spices and oil and mix well. Add the warm water and mix again to form a sticky but workable paste, then leave to rest uncovered for 10 minutes.

Place one spinach leaf vein-side up on a chopping board or work surface with the leaf tip furthest from you. Gently but thoroughly spread about 1½ teaspoons of the paste in a 5mm layer all over one side of the leaf, taking care not to tear it. Place a second leaf on top and repeat with the paste. Carefully lift the sides of the leaves and fold in to meet in the centre, then spread a layer of paste over the folded sections (the new top surface). Lift the closest end of the leaf and fold about 2cm onto itself, then repeat and continue to fold away from you until you reach the tip.

Place the rolled leaf seamside-down in an oiled pan or dish. Repeat this process until all 32 are pasted and folded.

Heat the 100ml of oil for the curry in a large thick-based pan on a medium heat for 1 minute, then add the mustard seeds. When they pop, add the carom seeds and fry for 30 seconds. Stir in the asafetida, then

CONTINUED OVERLEAF

1 tsp *garam masala*

4 tsp sunflower oil, plus more to oil pan/dish

100ml warm water

CURRY

Masala – crush together using a pestle and mortar (or a blender) to make a fine paste

4–5 fresh green chillies (ideally Kenyan), trimmed but not de-seeded

2–4 cloves of garlic, soaked and peeled

4cm root ginger, peeled and roughly chopped

pinch of salt

100ml sunflower oil

1 tsp mustard seeds

2 tsp carom seeds

½ tsp asafetida

4 courgettes (approx. 890g), washed and cut in ½cm dice

3½ tsp ground coriander

½ tsp ground cumin

2 tsp salt

1½ tsp sugar

1 tsp turmeric

2 handfuls coriander, washed and finely chopped

700ml boiling water

¼ tsp *garam masala*

stir through the courgettes. Add the masala paste, ground coriander, ground cumin, salt, sugar, turmeric and 1 handful of fresh coriander. Stir through, add 400ml of boiling water and cook covered on a medium heat for 12 minutes, stirring every few minutes. Then use the back of a ladle gently to squash about a third of the courgettes – this helps them to cook and gives you a nice mixture of textures. Cover and cook for another 7 minutes.

Stir in another 200ml of boiling water, then gently place all the spinach parcels in the curry. Cover and cook for 5 minutes. Very gently stir, reduce the heat to low, add the final 100ml of boiling water and cook for 14 minutes. Stir in the *garam masala*, remove the pan from the heat and leave to rest uncovered for 5 minutes before garnishing with the remaining fresh coriander.

This is great to eat on its own, just as it is, but can also be enjoyed with *baath* (page 213).

BHAGAT MUTHIA ‹ lentil dough ball curry

(V, WF, N)

In the regional finals of a competition I once took part in, the chef I was cooking against made this dish. I won the competition but these delicate chana dhal *dough balls coated in their rich sauce released such an amazing aroma and warm flavour from the cardamom seeds that I just had to try them.*

SERVES 6

MUTHIA DOUGH BALLS

Masala – crush together using a pestle and mortar (or a blender) to make a fine paste

8 fresh green chillies (ideally Kenyan), trimmed but not de-seeded

4cm root ginger, peeled and roughly chopped

pinch of salt

250g *chana dhal*, rinsed once then soaked in 1 ltr water for 24 hours

½ tsp turmeric

¼ tsp asafetida

1 handful fresh coriander, washed and finely chopped

½ onion, peeled and blended

1 cardamom pod, seeds only

2 tsp gram (chickpea) flour

1½ tsp salt

1 tsp ground coriander

½ tsp ground cumin

2 tsp sunflower oil, plus extra for deep-frying

CURRY

1 medium red-skinned (or othe waxy) potato, cut in 1cm dice

1.5 ltr boiling water

2 cardamom pods, seeds only

150ml sunflower oil

Drain away the excess water from the soaked *chana dhal* and then blend to a fine texture. Tip into a large mixing bowl and spread out. Add the masala paste, turmeric, asafetida, fresh coriander, blended onion, cardamom seeds, gram flour, salt, ground coriander, ground cumin and 2 teaspoons of sunflower oil. Using your hands, gently mix everything together. Take your time and mix lightly so that the spices fully infuse the *dhal* to give your dough a good, even flavour.

Once you have mixed everything together, make the dough into small (2½cm) balls of approximately 20g each and lay them in a tray. There should be approximately 36 dough balls.

Heat the frying oil – about 10cm deep – in a large pan over a high heat (or in a deep fat fryer, if you have one) and when you think it is hot enough, test the temperature by dropping a little of the dough into the oil. When it is up to temperature, the piece will quickly spring back up to float on the surface. Reduce the heat to medium.

Carefully place the dough balls in the hot oil and fry for 5 minutes until the outside is crispy and the middle is cooked. You will be breaking up a number of these dough balls later so it is OK to break one or two now to check they are cooked. Using a slotted spoon, remove the balls from the oil and place on absorbent kitchen towel. Repeat with the remaining balls, making sure you let the oil come back up to full heat in between batches, ensuring that there are no excess bits of dough left floating in the oil.

1 tsp mustard seeds
½ tsp asafetida
1½ medium onions, cut in 1cm dice
3 medium vine tomatoes, cut in
  ½cm dice
2½ tsp salt
1½ tsp medium red chilli powder
2¼ tsp *garam masala*
1 tsp turmeric
2 tsp ground coriander
½ tsp ground cumin
3cm root ginger, peeled and coarsely
  blended
1 handful fresh coriander,
  washed and finely chopped

Put the potato and the boiling water in a large deep pan over a high heat. Cook for 4 minutes, then add the cardamom seeds and simmer for 6 minutes or until the potatoes are half-cooked. Take off the heat and set to one side (do not drain).

Heat 150ml of sunflower oil in a thick-based frying pan for 2 minutes on a medium heat, then add the mustard seeds. Swirl the seeds through the oil and when they start to pop, add the asafetida and swirl again. Now add the onions and give everything a good stir. Cook on full heat for 4 minutes, then mix in the tomatoes and cook covered for 6 minutes, stirring once.

Take the frying pan off the heat and mix through the salt, chilli powder, *garam masala*, turmeric, ground coriander, ground cumin, blended ginger and fresh coriander.

Put the potato pan on a high heat and gently empty the frying pan contents into it. Take a ladle of cooking water and use it to rinse the frying pan into the potatoes, so you don't lose any flavour. Now put 12 broken-up dough balls into the pan and add the remaining 24 whole ones. Stir and cook uncovered for 8 minutes. Remove from the heat and leave to rest covered for 20 minutes.

Reheat on a medium heat until piping hot, and serve in large bowls with *bathura* (page 208) and *barela marcha* (page 243).

RAJASTHANI GATTA ⟨ Rajasthani dough ball curry

(V, WF, N)

We're very close to the team at Prashad – I consider them to be more like family, and we always know what is going on each other's lives. One of the chefs, Ramesh, is from Rajasthan, and this dish is inspired by him. He loves popping over with his boys to sample my version of this and other Rajasthani curries.

SERVES 4

GATTA DOUGH BALLS

200g gram (chickpea) flour, sieved
1 tsp carom seeds
½ tsp turmeric
1 tsp medium red chilli powder
1 tsp ground coriander
½ tsp ground cumin
½ tsp fruit salts (e.g. Eno or
  Andrews)
1 tsp salt
35ml sunflower oil
60ml warm water
1.5 ltr boiling water

CURRY

*Masala – crush together using
a pestle and mortar (or a blender)
to make a fine paste*
6–8 cloves of garlic, soaked and
  peeled
5cm root ginger, peeled and
  roughly chopped
pinch of salt

1 medium red-skinned (or other
  waxy) potato, cut in 2cm dice
150g cauliflower, cut into 2cm florets
80g French beans, topped, tailed
  and halved
75ml sunflower oil
4cm cinnamon
3 large Indian bay leaves, washed

Mix the gram flour, carom seeds, turmeric, chilli powder, ground coriander, ground cumin, fruit salts and salt in a large bowl. As the ingredients are dry, you will be able to really toss them around in the bowl and make sure everything is well mixed. Make a well in the middle and pour in the oil and warm water. Gently work the flour into the middle until it is all incorporated, then knead the dough. You will end up with a very tight mixture. Roll into 2cm-diameter balls of about 15g each and lay them in a baking tray. There should be roughly 21 dough balls.

Pour the boiling water into a deep pan on a high heat. Put the dough balls in the water. They will initially sink to the bottom but as they cook they will float to the top. After 6 minutes, scoop them out using a slotted spoon and lay them back on the tray.

Put the potato in the same boiling water for 7 minutes until half-cooked. Now add the cauliflower and French beans, cover and cook for 2 minutes. Take off the heat and drain.

Heat the 75ml of oil for the curry in a large thick-based frying pan on a medium heat for 2 minutes. Add the cinnamon and bay leaves and let them infuse the oil for a minute before adding the cumin seeds. Give them a swirl and as soon as they start to froth, add the asafetida, quickly followed by the onions and turn the heat to full. Cook the onions for 4 minutes, stirring regularly to make sure they get a good coating of the infused oil. Stir in the fresh red pepper slices, reduce the heat to medium and cook for 3 minutes, then stir in the

2 tsp cumin seeds
½ tsp asafetida
2 medium onions, cut in 1cm dice
½ large red pepper, cut into
  ½cm strips
4 vine tomatoes, blended to a
  smooth pulp
1 tsp medium red chilli powder
1 tsp *garam masala*
2 tsp ground coriander
½ tsp ground cumin
1 tsp turmeric
2 tsp salt
1 handful fresh coriander,
  washed and finely chopped
180ml boiling water

blended tomatoes and cook for a further minute. Add the masala paste, chilli powder, ground coriander, ground cumin, turmeric, salt and fresh coriander and fold through. Cover and cook for 5 minutes.

Finally add all the drained vegetables, the dough balls and the boiling water. Gently stir through, re-cover and cook for 6 minutes on a high heat, stirring occasionally. Take off the heat and leave to rest for 20 minutes uncovered.

Reheat on a medium heat until piping hot, and serve with *rotli* (page 206) and *mitu gajar murabho* (page 233).

SABZI & PANEER MAKNI ⟨ creamy *paneer* curry

(WF, N)

Paneer can be a bit of a challenge to work with but when cooked it has the most phenomenal texture. This tangy curry is Minal's variation on traditional paneer makni. *It's a really luxurious, creamy dish with a wonderful combination of spices.*

SERVES 4

Masala
3–4 cloves of garlic, soaked and
  peeled
4cm root ginger, peeled and roughly
  chopped
pinch of salt

sunflower oil for deep-frying,
  plus 100ml
365g *paneer* cheese, cut into 2cm
  x 1cm batons
6cm cinnamon stick
2 large Indian bay leaves, washed
4 cloves
6 whole black peppercorns
1 fresh cardamom pod, seeds only
1 medium onion, cut in ½cm dice
90g French beans, topped and tailed
  and cut in ½cm dice
6 chestnut mushrooms, cut in
  ½cm dice
1 tsp medium red chilli powder
1 tsp turmeric
2 tsp *garam masala*
2 tsp ground coriander
½ tsp ground cumin
2 tsp salt
1 handful fresh coriander,
  washed and finely chopped
7 medium vine tomatoes, washed
  and blended to a smooth pulp
60ml warm water
5 tsp double cream

Crush the garlic and ginger together with a pinch of salt using a pestle and mortar (or a blender), to make a fine masala paste.

Heat the frying oil – about 10cm deep – in a large pan over a high heat (or in a deep fat fryer, if you have one) and when you think it is hot enough, test the temperature by dropping a little *paneer* into the oil. When it is up to temperature, the *paneer* will quickly spring back up to float on the surface. Reduce the heat to medium. Carefully put the *paneer* batons in the hot oil and fry for 1 minute until they start to go brown at the edges and slightly crispy. As each one is ready, remove from the pan using a slotted spoon and place on absorbent kitchen towel until all the batons have been fried. Now put the *paneer* pieces into a bowl of cold water and leave to soak for 3 minutes. Remove from the water, squeeze the *paneer* gently with your hands to remove any remaining water, and place on a clean sheet of absorbent kitchen towel until needed.

Heat the 100ml of sunflower oil in a large thick-based frying pan on full heat for 1½ minutes. Add the cinnamon, bay leaves, cloves, peppercorns and cardamom and swirl them through the warm oil for about 40 seconds to let the spices release their magic. Add the onion and stir through. Cook for 2 minutes, then stir in the French beans and cook for a further 2 minutes. Add the mushrooms and cook for 1½ minutes.

CONTINUED OVERLEAF

Turn the heat down to medium, stir in the masala paste and cook for 1 minute. Increase the heat back to high, stir again and cook for 1½ minutes. Stir in the chilli powder, turmeric, *garam masala*, ground coriander, ground cumin, salt and half the fresh coriander, then the blended tomatoes, then the warm water. Simmer for 2 minutes.

Reduce the heat to medium again, cover and cook for 12 minutes, stirring every couple of minutes. Stir in the double cream, re-cover and cook for one more minute before removing from the heat and leaving to rest covered for 10 minutes.

Reheat on a medium heat until piping hot, sprinkle with the remaining fresh coriander and, if you're feeling traditional, serve with *palak puri* (page 219) and *baath* (page 213).

LIGHT LUNCHES
AND LEFTOVERS

SEV MOMRA BHEL ❦ puffed rice, potato and chickpea *chaat*

CHANA DHAL CHAAT ❦ Indian chickpea salad

BREAD BHAJIA ❦ Indian fried bread

DABELI ❦ mashed potato and chilli sandwich

PAV VADA ❦ spicy bread and potato patties

SABUDANA VADA ❦ tapioca, peanut and potato *bhajis*

MAKAI KHANDA VADA ❦ sweetcorn & onion *bhajis*

MAKAI CUTLETS ❦ semolina-encrusted sweetcorn *bhajis*

TUVAR DHOKRI VADA ❦ green pigeon pea and gram flour *bhajis*

PANEER SPHERES ❦ crispy cheese and potato balls

MAUSAMI TIKKI ❦ leek, broccoli, spinach and
asparagus croquettes

PALAK & PANEER GOOGRA ❦ cheesy spinach parcels

VAGARELA TORTILLAS ❦ spicy yoghurty tortillas

VAGARELA WATTANA ❦ spicy coconut peas

The school I went to in India was just across the road from our house and every day I'd run home at lunchtime (usually with several of my classmates in tow) to hungrily tuck into whatever delicious food my grandmother had prepared for us. My grandmother was an excellent cook and she often made lunch for the workers on the farm too. It was simple but filling fare – something to keep them going for the rest of the day. There would be several dishes, as is the Indian way, and everyone would have a bit of each one, chatting noisily, and then take a rest for an hour or so, while the sun cooled down. Then we'd all go back to school or work until the early evening.

Lunchtimes today, for most people at least, tend to be a bit more of a hurried affair – and few of us have the luxury of a quick nap! We eat more lightly now too, most likely due to the fact fewer of us work in manual roles. The recipes in this chapter are probably more familiar to you as dishes you've seen on the starters menu in a restaurant, or bought from a street food van. You may not traditionally see them as lunch food, but in our house, these are what make lunchtimes special. We can have a few light and delicious bites, without being weighed down by a full curry dish. Most of them are also very well-suited for packing away into a lunchbox and transporting to the office either to eat cold or to reheat in the microwave. Many Indian dishes, especially vegetarian ones, actually taste even better the next day, once their flavours have had a chance to infuse and deepen. You'll have already seen that there are several recipes in the book, like the *mung dhal* (page 73), that my sons love to eat cold for breakfast.

We often make use of leftovers from the night before, turning them into something new for lunch. Traditionally, these *vagarela* dishes (*vagarela* means to re-infuse) were a bit of a rarity, since almost every meal was cooked from scratch. It was exciting to see how, with a bit of magic in the kitchen, staples such as cooked rice or a few uneaten breads could be turned into a different delicious meal. More recently, *vagarela* dishes have become equally popular in Indian homes, but now it's because they are an efficient and economical way to whip up something quickly.

Not all of the recipes are super-speedy though; there are also a few dishes for when you have a bit of time midday to spend on cooking something special. And some of these recipes, like the *paneer* spheres (page 123) and the *bhajis* (pages 116–20) are really best eaten fresh from the pan, while they are still crispy and hot. These are great quick dishes for guests too. In Indian culture, we treat our guests like gods, and it's actually the custom to drop by unexpectedly. Anyone can be prepared with a clean house and something to eat if they know their sister and her husband are coming over two weeks on Wednesday, but surprise visitors are the true test of a host. We would never serve up a plate of leftovers to guests; only freshly cooked snacks will do – and preferably something fried and luxurious. It's all about showing your guests how welcome they are, and how you respect them. Lots of the recipes in this chapter are perfect for this.

Make a change from your usual sandwich or hastily grabbed salad box, and try lunch Gujarati-style.

SEV MOMRA BHEL ❧ puffed rice, potato and chickpea *chaat*

(V, N)

In the summer, my grandmother and I used to walk across the countryside a little way to the mango farm. There were fields full of the most beautiful mangoes growing on trees – small orange mangoes, huge red ones that were too heavy for me to carry, and so many amazing yellows and even pinks. The scent of sweet mango flesh takes me straight back to those precious warm early evenings. The freshness of the mango works really well with these bhels *and I'm proud to say that this is still one of the most popular dishes in the restaurant, even after twenty years.*

SERVES 4

100g chapatti flour, sieved

2 tsp sunflower oil, plus more to smooth the dough, oil the tray and for deep-frying

2 tsp lemon juice

¼ tsp salt

40ml warm water

2 tsp cumin seeds

300g plain live set yoghurt

3½ tsp sugar

400g *sev momra* (Indian vermicelli and rice puffs)

2 medium red-skinned (or other waxy) potatoes, peeled, boiled and cut in 1cm dice

1 x 400g tin chickpeas, drained and rinsed

1 large onion, cut in ½cm dice

1 handful fresh coriander, washed and finely chopped

200ml *imli* chutney (page 241), plus extra to drizzle on top

4 tsp *lasan* chutney (page 239)

1 small green mango, de-seeded, peeled and cut in ½cm dice

Use your hands to mix the flour, 2 teaspoons of sunflower oil, lemon juice, salt and warm water in a medium-sized bowl to form a stiff dough. Knead for a minute or so, then smooth the surface with a little oil and leave to rest for 15 minutes.

Split the dough in two. Roll half of it out on a lightly-floured work surface until about 2mm thick. Use a palette knife to cut it into rectangles of roughly 2cm x 1cm, placing them on a lightly-oiled tray as you go. Repeat with the other half of the dough.

Heat the frying oil – about 10cm deep – in a large pan over a high heat (or in a deep fat fryer, if you have one) and when you think it is hot enough, test the temperature by dropping a few pieces of the dough into the oil. When it is up to temperature, the pieces will quickly spring back up to float on the surface. Reduce the heat to medium.

Use a slotted spoon to transfer 10–12 dough rectangles to the oil (or fewer, depending on the size of your pan). Use a wooden or heatproof plastic spoon to move them around so that they cook evenly. Fry for a minute or two until they start to turn golden brown. Remove from the oil with the slotted spoon and place on absorbent kitchen towel while you fry the next batch. Repeat until all the dough has been fried, making sure

CONTINUED OVERLEAF

you let the oil come back up to full heat in between batches and that there are no excess bits of dough left floating in the oil.

Dry-roast the cumin seeds in a frying pan over a low heat for 1 minute, shaking the pan to toast them evenly, until they start to darken slightly. Finely crush the roasted seeds with a pestle and mortar or in a blender, then add to the yoghurt and sugar in a medium bowl and whisk the mixture until runny.

Mix the fried dough pieces, yoghurt mixture and all the other ingredients apart from the mango in a large bowl. Don't worry if some of the crispy bits start to break up.

Serve cold in small bowls, garnished with the mango.

CHANA DHAL CHAAT *Indian chickpea salad

(V, WF, N, HO)

This is a really refreshing and crunchy dish, full of vibrant flavours and textures. It is important to eat it as soon as you have finished mixing everything together, as otherwise the roasted chana dhal *will lose its crunchiness. You can buy ready-made roasted spiced* chana dhal *as a healthy(ish) snack in most Indian grocery stores and online. In India, versions of this salad are sold at the streetside in paper cones for a speedy bite to eat while on-the-go.*

SERVES 4

600g spicy roasted *chana dhal* snack
2 medium onions, cut in ½cm dice
1 handful fresh coriander, washed and finely chopped
3 fresh green chillies (ideally Kenyan), seeded and finely chopped
juice of ½ lemon
1 vine medium tomato, washed and cut in 1cm dice

Mix all the ingredients in a bowl and serve cold – simple but delicious. This tastes particularly good with a sweet cup of *masala chai* (page 247).

BREAD BHAJIA · Indian fried bread

(V, N)

This is a bit of a mixture of ideas drawn from a range of cuisines and it illustrates well how our cooking at home has been influenced by all the different cultures around us. It is an Indian take on Chinese prawn toasts, but made with a very English mashed potato topping. It's very satisfying, especially on a cold day – Bobby is particularly keen on them! It's also a great way of using up leftover mash.

SERVES 4-5

8–10 slices of white bread

Masala
6–8 fresh green chillies (ideally Kenyan)
2–4 cloves of garlic, soaked and peeled
2½cm root ginger, peeled
pinch of salt

Topping
3 medium red-skinned (or other waxy) potatoes, peeled, boiled and mashed (about 550g)
1 handful fresh coriander, washed and finely chopped
1¼ tsp salt
1½ tsp sugar
pinch turmeric
juice of ½ lemon

Batter
150g gram (chickpea) flour, sieved
1 tsp salt
1 tsp medium red chilli powder
2 tsp lemon juice
200ml water

sunflower oil for deep-frying

Cut the crusts off the bread and cut each slice into 4 triangles. Crush the chillies, garlic and ginger together with a pinch of salt using a pestle and mortar (or a blender), to make a fine masala paste.

Mix the topping ingredients and the masala paste together in a large bowl, making sure the potato picks up all the flavours along the way. Whisk together the flour, salt, chilli powder, lemon juice and water in a separate bowl to make a runny batter.

Heat the frying oil – about 10cm deep – in a large pan over a high heat (or in a deep fat fryer, if you have one) and when you think it is hot enough, test the temperature by dropping a little of the batter into the oil. When it is up to temperature, the batter will quickly spring back up to float on the surface. Reduce the heat to medium.

Taking one triangle of bread at a time, put 3–4 teaspoons of potato mixture on top, pat down and drizzle with batter. Carefully place in the oil and fry for around 50–60 seconds, until the bread-side is golden and crispy. Remove from the oil with a slotted spoon and place on absorbent kitchen towel while you prepare the next slice. Repeat with the rest of the bread, making sure you let the oil come back up to full heat in between slices.

Serve immediately with *vagarela beans* (page 136).

DABELI ⟨ mashed potato and chilli sandwich

(GO)

The Gujarati diet includes a lot of bread, with flatbreads or chapatis piled high on the table at almost every meal, ready for scooping up every last drop of delicious curry sauce. This recipe is another great Indian street food style dish, but it is influenced by the soft white bread we have come to love since living in the UK. Eat it on its own to appreciate all the layers of flavour and different textures.

SERVES 4

50ml sunflower oil

1 tsp cumin seeds

4 medium red-skinned (or other waxy) potatoes, boiled, peeled and mashed

½ tsp turmeric

1½ tsp medium red chilli powder

2 tsp ground coriander

2 tsp ground cumin

2 tsp *garam masala*

2 tsp salt

juice of ½ lime

12 finger bread buns, sliced in half and generously buttered

200ml *imli* chutney (page 241)

25g salted peanuts, coarsely ground

1 medium red onion, cut in ½cm dice

2 medium vine tomatoes, cut in ½cm dice

1 handful fresh coriander, washed and finely chopped

melted butter (about 5g) to brush the buns

40g *sev* (Indian chickpea vermicelli)

Heat the oil in a large thick-based frying pan on a high heat for 1½ minutes. Add the cumin seeds, and when they start to bubble, use a wooden or heatproof plastic spoon to stir in the mashed potato, ensuring it gets well coated in the cumin-infused oil. Reduce the heat to low and add the turmeric, chilli powder, ground coriander, ground cumin, *garam masala,* salt and lime. Mix everything together and cook for 2½ minutes. Take off the heat.

Using a griddle pan, gently toast the buttered buns on both sides. Everyone can then make their own layered sandwich by generously filling a bun with *imli* chutney, some potato mixture and a sprinkling of ground peanuts, garnished with chopped red onion, chopped vine tomatoes and fresh coriander. Close the lid of your bun, brush the top with a little butter and sprinkle with *sev* before tucking in.

PAV VADA *c* spicy bread and potato patties

(V, WF, N)

I used to fry these as a welcome-home-from-school snack for my children, but they make a warming lunch too with a simple salad – and maybe some ketchup! They are a popular Indian street food and the aromas from the spices, released when you cook the patties, immediately transport me to a busy Bombay marketday. Be warned though: these can be a bit on the spicy side, so I've given a wide range of chilli and garlic quantities to suit your audience. Don't worry if the bread is a bit stale, it's actually better for adding texture.

SERVES 6

Masala
4–10 fresh green chillies (ideally
  Kenyan)
3–7 cloves of garlic, soaked and
  peeled
1½cm root ginger, peeled
pinch of salt

3 medium white baps or 4 slices
  white bread
3 medium red-skinned (or other
  waxy) potatoes, boiled,
  peeled and mashed (about
  500–600g)
2 handfuls fresh coriander,
  washed and finely chopped
1½ tsp salt
2 tsp sugar
4 tsp sesame seeds
4 tsp bottled or fresh lemon juice
sunflower oil for deep-frying

Crush the chillies, garlic and ginger together with a pinch of salt using a pestle and mortar (or a blender), to make a fine masala paste.

Slice the bread (if not already sliced) and dip in cold water for a couple of seconds. Squeeze tightly to remove all the excess water, then place in a mixing bowl with the mashed potato. Add the masala paste, fresh coriander, salt, sugar, sesame seeds and lemon juice and mix everything together to create a pâté-style mixture. You'll find that the bread breaks up easily.

Rub a little oil onto the palms of your hands and make the mixture into 6cm diameter balls. Gently flatten them into discs around 1cm thick. This should make around 18–20 patties.

Heat the frying oil – about 10cm deep – in a large pan over a high heat (or in a deep fat fryer) and when you think it is hot enough, test the temperature by dropping a little of the mixture into the oil. When it is up to temperature, the mixture will quickly spring back up to float on the surface. Reduce the heat to medium.

Carefully place 4 patties at a time in the hot oil and fry for 2½ minutes, stirring with a wooden or heatproof plastic spoon until golden brown. Remove them from the oil with a slotted spoon and place on absorbent kitchen towel. Repeat with the remaining patties, making sure you let the oil come back up to full heat in between batches.

Serve immediately with a bit of ketchup to dip them in, a leafy salad and some *barela marcha* (page 243) for a little extra sweet chilli heat.

SABUDANA VADA ~ tapioca, peanut and potato *bhajis*
(V, WF)

This may sound like a bit of an unusual combination of ingredients but the peanuts give these little fried treats a wonderful texture. Everyone is familiar with onion bhajis, usually served as a starter or as part of a spread of dishes, but these potato versions make a delicious and surprisingly filling light lunch with just a fresh salad alongside.

SERVES 4

Masala
6–8 fresh green chillies (ideally
  Kenyan)
4–6 cloves of garlic, soaked
  and peeled
pinch of salt

200g tapioca
200ml warm water
135g red-skinned (unroasted,
  unsalted) peanuts, finely chopped
  or blended
4 medium red-skinned (or other
  waxy) potatoes, peeled, boiled
  and mashed (about 700g)
1 handful fresh coriander,
  washed and finely chopped
2¾ tsp salt
2 tsp sugar
10 tsp lemon juice
sunflower oil for deep-frying

Soak the tapioca in the warm water for 10–12 minutes. Crush the chillies and garlic together with a pinch of salt using a pestle and mortar (or a blender), to make a fine masala paste.

Toast the chopped peanuts in a frying pan on a medium heat for 4 minutes, swirling and tossing them in the pan every 30 seconds or so. Take off the heat and leave in the pan for 10 minutes to cool.

Use your hands to mix the cooled peanuts, masala paste, mashed potato, fresh coriander, salt, sugar and lemon juice together in a large bowl, working the flavours through the potato. Drain the tapioca and lightly mix it in, again using your hands, being careful not to squash it. Form into discs approximately 6cm in diameter and 1½ cm thick.

Heat the frying oil – about 10cm deep – in a large pan over a high heat (or in a deep fat fryer) and when you think it is hot enough, test the temperature by dropping a small piece of the mixture into the oil. When it is up to temperature, the mixture will quickly spring up to the surface. Reduce the heat to medium.

Using a slotted spoon, carefully place as many discs as will comfortably fit into your pan in the hot oil and fry for 45 seconds before flipping over and cooking for a further 1½ minutes until golden brown. Remove them from the oil with a slotted spoon and place on absorbent kitchen towel. Repeat with the remaining discs, making sure you let the oil come back up to full heat in between batches and that there are no excess bits of dough left floating in the oil.

Serve immediately (before they go soft) with *shimla mirch* (page 237).

MAKAI KHANDA VADA ⟨ sweetcorn & onion *bhajis*

(V, WF, N)

One of Mohan's favourite vegetables is sweetcorn and he loves to eat these bhajis *in the summer, as they're very light and sweet. Try them with a generous spoonful of* imli *chutney (page 241), and if you're at home and have the time, they also go really well with some freshly cooked* masala *chips (page 224).*

SERVES 4

Masala
4–6 fresh green chillies (ideally Kenyan)
2–4 cloves of garlic, soaked and peeled
1cm root ginger, peeled
pinch of salt

1 x 340g tin sweetcorn, coarsely blended with the juice
1 medium onion, cut in ¾cm dice
1½ tsp salt
1 handful fresh coriander, washed and finely chopped
pinch of turmeric
750g gram (chickpea) flour, sieved
sunflower oil for deep-frying

Crush the chillies, garlic and ginger together with a pinch of salt using a pestle and mortar (or a blender), to make a fine masala paste.

Use your hands to mix the blended sweetcorn, onion, masala paste, salt, coriander, turmeric and half the gram flour in a large bowl until well combined – I work in half the flour at a time to avoid ending up with lumpy dough. Add the rest of the gram flour and continue to mix with your hands until it is fully incorporated. The dough should be reasonably loose but able to hold together when squeezed. Use your hands to form it into 5cm diameter discs (it should make 16–18) and set aside.

Heat the frying oil – about 10cm deep – in a large pan over a high heat (or in a deep fat fryer, if you have one) and when you think it is hot enough, test the temperature by dropping a little of the dough into the oil. When it is up to temperature, the dough will quickly spring back up to float on the surface. Reduce the heat to medium.

Using a slotted spoon, carefully place as many discs as will comfortably fit into your pan in the hot oil and fry for 30 seconds before flipping over and cooking for a further 5 minutes until golden brown. Remove them from the oil with a slotted spoon and place on absorbent kitchen towel to rest for at least 2 minutes. Repeat with the remaining discs, making sure you let the oil come back up to full heat in between batches and that there are no excess bits of dough left floating in the oil.

Serve immediately piping hot with *imli chutney* (page 241) and *masala* chips (page 224).

MAKAI CUTLETS & semolina-encrusted sweetcorn *bhajis*
(V, N)

A great little snack or light lunch that makes good use of ingredients and leftovers. As I've said before: feel no shame in saving time where you can – tinned sweetcorn is a fantastic shortcut. I used to have to scrape off all the kernels from a fresh corncob, but nowadays we don't have to. The semolina coating gives these a lovely crunch and they look beautiful on the plate.

SERVES 4-5

Masala
4–6 fresh green chillies (ideally
  Kenyan)
4–6 cloves of garlic, soaked
  and peeled
4cm root ginger, peeled
pinch of salt

25ml sunflower oil, plus more
  for frying
1 red pepper, cut in ½cm dice
1 medium onion, cut in ½cm dice
3 medium red-skinned (or other
  waxy) potatoes, boiled, peeled
  and cooled
1 x 340g tin sweetcorn, drained
  and coarsely blended
½ handful fresh coriander,
  washed and finely chopped
3 tsp salt
2 tsp cumin seeds
juice of 1 lime
40g cornflour, sieved
75g coarse semolina, plus extra
  to line the tray
mixed leaf salad, to serve
olive oil, to drizzle

Crush the chillies, garlic and ginger together with a pinch of salt using a pestle and mortar (or a blender), to make a fine masala paste.

Heat the oil in a large thick-based frying pan on a high heat for 30 seconds. Add the pepper, reduce the heat to low and cook for 40 seconds. Add the onion, increase the heat to medium and fry for 2½ minutes. Set aside.

Grate the potatoes into a large mixing bowl, then add the masala paste. Pick up handfuls of the blended sweetcorn and squeeze out as much water as possible before adding to the potatoes. Then add the cooked peppers and onions along with the fresh coriander, salt, cumin seeds, lime juice and cornflour and lightly mix everything together. Leave the mixture to cool for half an hour, then lightly oil your hands and make the mixture into balls of approximately 45g each (about 27 balls in total). Toss each ball in the semolina and gently press to make a slightly oval shape. Lay the balls in a semolina-lined tray.

Heat the frying oil – about 10cm deep – in a large pan over a high heat (or in a deep fat fryer) and when you think it is hot enough, test the temperature by dropping a little mixture into the oil. When it is up to temperature, the mixture will quickly spring up to the surface. Reduce the heat to medium. Using a slotted spoon, carefully place 4 balls at a time in the hot oil and fry for 1½ minutes. Remove them with a slotted spoon and place on absorbent kitchen towel. Repeat with the remaining balls, making sure you let the oil come back up to full heat in between batches.

Garnish with the fresh coriander and serve immediately on a bed of mixed leaf salad drizzled with olive oil.

TUVAR DHOKRI VADA ⟨ green pigeon pea and gram flour *bhajis* (V, WF, N)

As well as being a fantastic cook, my grandmother was also a very generous woman. Tradespeople, neighbours, friends of mine and often even strangers, all tempted in by the wonderful smells from the kitchen, were warmly welcomed at the table. I was making these bhajis *one day when the windowcleaner popped his head around the door and I invited him in to try some: from a rural village in India to Bradford, people are all the same. These are best enjoyed with a dip, like* safarjan wattana *(page 238) or a good tomato salsa.*

SERVES 6

Masala
4–7 fresh green chillies (ideally Kenyan)
2–4 cloves of garlic, soaked and peeled
6cm root ginger, peeled
pinch of salt

450g frozen green pigeon peas (or petits pois), thawed
1.1 ltr boiling water
2½ tsp salt
3½ tsp sugar
3 tsp ground coriander
½ tsp ground cumin
½ tsp turmeric
250g gram (chickpea) flour, sieved
100g cornmeal flour, sieved
sunflower oil for deep-frying

Crush the chillies, garlic and ginger together with a pinch of salt using a pestle and mortar (or a blender), to make a fine masala paste.

Wash the thawed pigeon peas and pick out any slightly yellow, overripe ones as they won't cook properly. Put the peas into 900ml of the boiling water in a large pan and simmer for 30 minutes. Take off the heat and gently mash the peas in the water remaining in the pan – don't completely blend them; keep some texture.

Place the peas back on the heat and add the remaining 200ml of boiling water along with the salt, sugar, ground coriander, ground cumin, turmeric and masala paste. Stir through and cook for 2 minutes.

Mix in the gram flour and cornmeal flour and keep stirring on a medium heat, working the dough round the pan for 2–3 minutes. You might need to scrape it off the back of the spoon to help work it around the pan. Reduce the heat to low and continue mixing for a minute, then cover and cook for 2 minutes. Give it another quick stir, then re-cover and cook for a further 4 minutes.

Spread the dough on a large baking tray to allow it to cool. While it cools, check your pan – it may be looking a little bit tired by now; you'll find it easier to clean if you fill it with boiling water and a teaspoon of salt and leave to soak for a while before washing up. As soon as the dough is cool enough to handle, use your hands to make it into 1cm patties.

Heat the frying oil – about 10cm deep – in a large pan over a high heat (or in a deep fat fryer, if you have one) and when you think it is hot enough, test the temperature by dropping a small piece of the dough into the oil. When it is up to temperature, the dough will quickly spring back up to float on the surface. Reduce the heat to medium.

Using a slotted spoon, carefully place as many patties as will comfortably fit into your pan in the hot oil and fry for 1½ minutes before flipping over and cooking for a further 4 minutes. Remove them from the oil with a slotted spoon and place on absorbent kitchen towel. Repeat with the remaining patties, making sure you let the oil come back up to full heat in between batches and also remove excess bits of dough which are floating in the oil.

Serve piping hot with *chana chaat patti* (page 244) and *safarjan wattana* (page 238) for a great combination of hot and cold delights.

PANEER SPHERES ‹ crispy cheese and potato balls

(N)

People dropping by unexpectedly, as is the Hindu custom, are the true test for a generous host. You must offer them something to eat, and it can't just be a bowl of leftovers and a cup of tea. Your guests should be treated like gods: only the best will do. Make a fresh batch of these creamy, hot, luxurious deep-fried snacks to show how welcome they are. They also make a lovely warming lunch with a salad.

SERVES 4-5

1 large medium red-skinned
  (or other waxy) potato, boiled,
  peeled and cooled
425g *paneer* cheese, grated
4–6 fresh green chillies (ideally
  Kenyan), finely chopped
4–6 cloves of garlic, finely chopped
2 tsp salt
2 tsp coarsely ground black pepper
juice of 1½ limes
40g cornflour, sieved
75g coarse semolina, plus extra
  to line the tray
sunflower oil for deep-frying
½ handful fresh coriander,
  washed and finely chopped
mixed leaf salad, to serve
olive oil, to drizzle

Grate the potato and *paneer* into a large bowl. Mix together, lifting the potato and cheese strands through each other. Add the chillies, garlic, salt, pepper, lime juice and cornflour and gently mix everything together, making sure you don't squash the potato and *paneer* so that the mixture retains some texture.

Leave to cool for half an hour, then lightly oil your hands and make into 4cm-diameter balls of approximately 35g each (about 27 balls in total). Toss each ball in the semolina and gently press to make a slightly oval shape. Lay the balls in a semolina-lined tray.

Heat the oil – about 10cm deep – in a large pan over a high heat (or in a deep fat fryer, if you have one) and when you think it is hot enough, test the temperature by dropping a little of the mixture into the oil. When the oil is up to temperature, the mixture will quickly spring back up to float on the surface. Reduce the heat to medium.

Using a slotted spoon, carefully place 4 balls at a time in the hot oil and fry for 1½ minutes until golden brown. Remove them from the oil with a slotted spoon and place on absorbent kitchen towel. Repeat with the remaining balls, making sure you let the oil come back up to full heat in between batches.

Garnish with the fresh coriander and serve immediately on a bed of mixed leaf salad drizzled with olive oil, with some *safarjan wattana* (page 238) alongside.

MAUSAMI TIKKI ⟨ leek, broccoli, spinach and asparagus croquettes (V, OG, N)

Like the paneer *spheres (page 123), these delicately spiced croquettes are quick and easy, making them perfect for impromptu guests, and you can easily swap the green veggies for any you may already have. Asparagus isn't a traditional Indian ingredient, but my daughter-in-law, Minal, loves to cook with it, as it soaks up spices in a really special way. Serve with a salad, and they go particularly well with a dip like* kopru *(page 235), some* barela marcha *(page 243) and if you're feeling a bit hungrier,* masala *chips (page 224).*

SERVES 4

30ml sunflower oil, plus extra
  for deep–frying
1 tsp cumin seeds
180g broccoli, finely chopped
200g leeks, finely chopped
7 green asparagus spears,
  trimmed and grated
10 spinach leaves without stems,
  washed and finely chopped
2 large red-skinned (or other
  waxy) potatoes, boiled,
  peeled and cooled
2–4 fresh green chillies (ideally
  Kenyan), finely chopped
1 tsp red chilli flakes
½ handful fresh coriander,
  washed and finely chopped
2 tsp salt
½ tsp coarsely ground
  black pepper
juice of ½ lime
4 tsp cornflour, sieved
75g coarse semolina, plus extra
  to line the tray

Heat 30ml of oil in a large thick-based frying pan on a high heat for 1½ minutes. Add the cumin seeds, and when they start to bubble, add the broccoli and fry for 30–40 seconds. Add the leeks and fry for 30 seconds, then add the grated asparagus and fry for 40 seconds. Take off the heat and stir in the finely chopped spinach. Spread the vegetables out on a plate or tray and leave to cool.

Grate the potatoes into a large mixing bowl. Add the chillies, chilli flakes, fresh coriander, salt, pepper, lime juice, cornflour and all the cooked vegetables. Gently mix everything together. Taste and season if required.

Lightly oil your hands and form the mixture into 3cm diameter balls. This should make about 16 balls. Toss each ball in the semolina and gently press to make a slightly oval shape. Lay the balls in a semolina-lined tray.

Heat the frying oil – about 10cm deep – in a large pan over a high heat (or in a deep fat fryer, if you have one) and when you think it is hot enough, test the temperature by dropping a little of the mixture into the oil. When it is up to temperature, the mixture will quickly spring back up to float on the surface. Reduce the heat to medium.

Using a slotted spoon, carefully place 4 balls at a time in the hot oil and fry for 1½ minutes until golden brown. Remove them from the oil with a slotted spoon and place on absorbent kitchen towel. Repeat with the remaining balls, making sure you let the oil come back up to full heat in between batches.

Serve immediately. I like to eat these with a red onion and rocket salad and some *safarjan wattana* (page 238).

PALAK & PANEER GOOGRA ⟨ cheesy spinach parcels

(N)

These little pastry pies with their warming spices and chillies are a deliciously gooey Indian take on that classic pairing. Serve them as soon as they are cooked, while the pastry is still crunchy and the filling rich and melted. I also recommend a spoonful of cooling relish, such as shimla mirch *(page 237), to go alongside.*

SERVES 4

Masala
3–5 fresh green chillies (ideally Kenyan)
2–4 cloves of garlic, soaked and peeled
pinch of salt

Filling
25ml sunflower oil
1 tsp cumin seeds
100g spinach, finely chopped
1 tsp salt
½ handful fresh coriander, washed and finely chopped
1 tsp *garam masala*
½ tsp turmeric
1 tsp ground coriander
pinch of ground cumin
170g *paneer* cheese, grated
juice of ¼ lime

Googra
1 tsp salt
1 tsp carom seeds
395g plain flour, sieved
25ml sunflower oil, plus more for deep-frying
150ml warm water

Crush the chillies and garlic with the salt using a pestle and mortar (or a blender), to make a fine masala paste.

To make the filling, heat the oil in a large thick-based frying pan on a high heat for 1½ minutes. Swirl the cumin seeds in the oil for 15 seconds. Reduce the heat to low, then stir in the spinach, masala paste, salt, fresh coriander, *garam masala* and turmeric. Add the ground coriander and ground cumin and stir for 40 seconds. Take off the heat and gently mix through the grated paneer. Add the lime juice and stir together lightly. Set aside.

Mix together the salt, carom seeds and flour in a large bowl. Mix through the oil, then add the warm water and knead to a firm dough. Break into 16 balls (about 30g each) and use a rolling pin to flatten each one into a 12cm-diameter disc. Place 20g of the filling in the middle of a disc, then fold into a half-moon and pinch the edges together. Ensure it is properly sealed by laying it on the table and pressing the edges with a fork – be careful not to pierce the dough. Repeat until all the parcels are stuffed and sealed. Lay them in a tray and cover with a tea towel so that they don't dry out.

Heat the frying oil – about 10cm deep – in a large pan over a high heat (or in a deep fat fryer) and when you think it is hot enough, test the temperature by dropping a little of the dough into the oil; it should quickly spring back up to float on the surface. Reduce the heat to medium. Fry a few parcels at a time in the hot oil for 2 minutes until light and crispy. Remove with a slotted spoon and place on absorbent kitchen towel. Repeat with the remaining parcels, making sure you let the oil come back up to heat between batches. Serve immediately with *shimla mirch* (page 237).

VAGARELA TORTILLAS ~ spicy yoghurty tortillas
(N, HO)

Early in the morning, just after sunrise, my grandmother and I often went down to the fields where the sorghum wheat grew, which was used to make rotli *and other breads. There were ears of golden corn several metres high, and if we weren't careful, the birds would eat it all before harvest time. We threw stones and made loud sounds as we chased the birds away. Grandma always brought snacks with us, usually wraps made from leftover breads. This is another great way of using up leftover wraps and breads as they soak up all the tasty spices, but you can also use pitta breads. Serve on its own, or with some of the other dishes in this chapter for more of a feast.*

SERVES 4

Masala
4–6 fresh green chillies (ideally Kenyan)
2–3 cloves of garlic, soaked and peeled
4cm root ginger, peeled
pinch of salt

8 x 25cm flour or corn tortillas
75ml sunflower oil
1 tsp fenugreek seeds
1 tsp mustard seeds
½ tsp turmeric
1¼ tsp salt
1¼ tsp sugar
2 handfuls fresh coriander, washed and finely chopped
125g plain live set yoghurt
1.1 ltr warm water

Crush the chillies, garlic and ginger together with a pinch of salt using a pestle and mortar (or a blender), to make a fine masala paste.

Tear the tortillas into roughly 4cm square pieces. Heat the oil in a large, deep frying pan on a medium heat for 2 minutes. Add the fenugreek seeds and mustard seeds, and when the mustard seeds start to pop, add the tortillas, frying for 2 minutes on each side in the spice-infused oil. Then add the masala paste, turmeric, salt and sugar and stir, gently frying the tortillas for 3 minutes each side. Add one handful of the fresh coriander and stir through for 3 minutes. Watch out for the mustard seeds, which may smoke and pop when dry-fried like this.

Now add the yoghurt and water to the pan and stir through gently, mixing the thick yoghurt into the spicy oil and covering the tortillas. Take off the heat and leave to stand for 2 minutes.

Serve immediately, garnished with the remaining fresh coriander.

VAGARELA WATTANA ~ spicy coconut peas

(W, F, HO)

This dry, sweet dish brings together all the flavours of 'real India' for me: chillies, garlic, coconut and coriander. It makes my mouth water just thinking about it! Spoon it into large bowls for a low-key lunch – maybe in front of a Bollywood film...

SERVES 4

Masala
4–6 fresh green chillies (ideally Kenyan)
4–6 cloves of garlic, soaked and peeled
3cm root ginger, peeled
pinch of salt

about 680–690g sugarsnap peas, in their pods
100ml sunflower oil
1 tsp mustard seeds
2 tsp carom seeds
$\frac{1}{3}$ tsp asafetida
250g frozen petits pois peas, thawed
2 tsp salt
1½ tsp turmeric
3 tsp sesame seeds
50g fresh coconut, shredded (or coarse desiccated coconut)
2 handfuls fresh coriander, washed and finely chopped
lemon wedges

Crush the chillies, garlic and ginger together with a pinch of salt using a pestle and mortar (or a blender), to make a fine masala paste.

Rinse the sugarsnaps and remove the strings from along their seams so that they can open up during cooking and absorb more of the wonderful flavours.

Heat the oil in a thick-based frying pan on a medium heat for 2 minutes. Add the mustard seeds and when they start to pop, add the carom seeds and asafetida and swirl them into the oil. Add the sugarsnap peas and petits pois and stir through the infused oil. Add the salt, turmeric, masala paste, sesame seeds, coconut and 1 handful of the fresh coriander. Stir through, cover and cook for 10 minutes, stirring halfway. Give the mixture another a good stir, then take off the heat and leave to rest for about 5 minutes uncovered.

Garnish with the remaining fresh coriander and serve with lemon wedges to squeeze over.

INDIAN FUSION

VAGARELA BEANS ❧ curried baked beans

CHEESE & AJMO TOAST ❧ green chilli pizza toast

SPICY VEGGIE BURGERS

SPICY PEA AND POTATO PASTIES

SPICY VEGGIE PIE

INDO-ITALIAN MACARONI CHEESE

INDO-ITALIAN VEGGIE LASAGNE

INDO-ITALIAN VEGGIE CANNELLONI

PANEER RAVIOLI

SPICY MUSHROOM AND PEPPER PIZZA

CHILLI PANEER ❧ Indo-Chinese marinated cheese stir-fry

CHINESE BHEL ❧ Indo-Chinese street-style rice and noodles

HAKKA NOODLES ❧ Indo-Chinese street food noodles

SZECHUAN RICE ❧ Indo-Chinese fried rice

MANCHURIAN CABBAGE DOUGH BALLS WITH
VEGETABLE STIR-FRY

MANCHOW SOUP ❧ hot and spicy stir-fry soup

INDO-MEXICAN VEGGIE ENCHILADAS

CHANA DHAL VADA ❧ Indian-style 'falafel' in toasted pitta

SAFFRON & GINGER PANNA COTTA

I think this actually may be my favourite chapter in the book. It showcases what cooking in our home is all about: the coming together of different cultures and cuisines. Whilst my family's Gujarati roots are very important to us, as a chef it's hard not to be inspired by all the wonderful food around me. My husband, Mohan, and I came to live in the UK when I was fifteen and he was sixteen. Back then, it wasn't easy to get hold of some the ingredients we were used to cooking with, and so we often had to make do with what was available – replacing fresh mango with Bramley apples and colcasia leaves with chard. In this way, those traditional Indian recipes I knew so well quickly evolved to suit my new life, and you'll have seen lots of examples of this throughout this book. But there were also many new styles of cooking to experience. With so much choice around us – then as well as now – my favourite aspects of different cuisines have found their way very happily into my kitchen.

The children – as all children do – loved it when I cooked something different for them. They were so excited when I didn't cook curry! Being so used to the lovely warm spices, though, I often had to find ways to include them, and that's how many of the dishes in this chapter originally came about. As most people who have young children to feed will appreciate, I am not against using a few shortcuts here and there either, and so there's even a recipe for baked beans on toast (Indian-style, of course), which was always Bobby's favourite.

Perhaps surprisingly, Italian cuisine is very interesting to an Indian chef and there are quite a few examples in this chapter of my take on those classic Italian dishes. You have to be quite careful adding the cheese that is never far away in an Italian meal, as it tends to dull the spices, but tomato sauces are a dream to work with. Mexican food, which combines tomatoes, cheese and chilli very successfully, has also taught me a lot about matching ingredients. I'm not sure how well known Indo-Chinese cuisine is outside of India but it is hugely popular *within* India, especially as street food. Mayur, my youngest son, is now championing street food in his own bar venture, Bundobust, in Leeds – I love how food connects us all together like this, coming almost full circle back to those dishes I first cooked when I arrived in the UK. I've included examples of each of these types of food over the following pages for you to try.

I owe a lot to my lovely daughter-in-law, Minal, too. There is a saying in India that when people are family, but they feel like 'more than family', when you just feel it is 'meant to be', it's because they are souls from a previous life who were related and who have found each other again. I think of this every time I look at Bobby and Minal together; we have been so lucky with the marriages in our family. Minal is very talented in the kitchen and she has taken many of my recipes and given them a twist of her own; as our family grows, we love to learn from each other and try out new ideas.

To me, fusion cuisine is the future. As you'll see, this isn't about simply throwing a few chopped chillies on top of a pizza; it's about bringing flavours together in inventive ways, mixing cultures to create some truly magical combinations. There are those who fear that the distinct characteristics of some traditional dishes will be lost, but personally I feel that what results from this coming together of ideas is something new and very special.

VAGARELA BEANS ⟨ curried baked beans

(V, WF, N)

You can't get more British than beans on toast! In this twist on the classic, I have simply added the same masala spice paste that I use in most of my Gujarati cooking to add some warmth and depth. Instead of serving these on top of toast, you could try them with bread bhajia *(page 111),* kobi pura *(page 36) or some spicy pea and potato pasties (page 140). My son Bobby enjoys eating these almost as much as he did when he was six years old, much to the dismay of his wife Minal, a chef with Michelin star ambitions.*

SERVES 4

Masala
4–6 fresh green chillies (ideally
  Kenyan)
4 cloves of garlic, soaked and
  peeled
pinch of salt

50ml sunflower oil
4 tsp carom seeds
2 x 400g tins baked beans
100ml water
cheese, to serve
black pepper, to serve

Crush the chillies and garlic together with a pinch of salt using a pestle and mortar (or a blender), to make a fine masala paste.

Heat the oil in a thick-based pan on a medium heat for 2 minutes. Swirl the carom seeds through the oil for 20 seconds until they start gently bubbling. Add the masala paste and keep stirring for 1 minute.

Pour the baked beans into the pan and swirl through the spice-infused oil. Use the 100ml water to rinse both tins into the pan, to minimise waste and maximise flavour. Cook uncovered for 4–5 minutes or until the sauce thickens slightly.

Serve piping hot with a few slices of unbuttered toast. Grate over some cheese and some ground pepper to finish it off.

CHEESE & AJMO TOAST & green chilli pizza toast

(OG, N)

A British staple, sliced bread, an Italian idea and Indian flavours: this is such a mix of cultures and I love it! Its simplicity really shows off how even just a subtle use of spices can totally transform a dish. Feel free to add your own toppings, such as sliced mushrooms or chopped spring onions, before you scatter over the cheese.

SERVES 4

12 slices white or brown bread
4 tsp carom seeds
2 tsp medium red chilli powder
185g tomato ketchup
350g mature Cheddar cheese,
   grated
8 green chillies (ideally Kenyan),
   finely sliced

Lightly toast the bread on both sides under the grill; slightly less on the side you are going to put the cheese on.

Mix the carom seeds and chilli powder with the tomato ketchup in a bowl and divide between the slices of toast, spreading up to the edges. Generously cover each with cheese and sprinkle with green chillies. Toast under the grill until the cheese is bubbling.

Serve immediately, piping hot.

SPICY VEGGIE BURGERS (V, OG, N)

Growing up in India, there were always people in the house: friends of my grandmother's, neighbours, even people who called at the door to sell vegetables would all be welcomed in for something to eat. And what could be a better meeting of Indian and British cultures than a barbecue? Even in the temperamental climate of Bradford. The potato and coarsely blended vegetables give these a denser texture than most other veggie burgers, so you really won't miss the meat.

MAKES 8 BURGERS

Masala
4–6 fresh green chillies (ideally Kenyan)
2cm root ginger, peeled
pinch of salt

2 medium red-skinned (or other waxy) potatoes, boiled, peeled and cooled
100g frozen peas, thawed and coarsely blended
1 green pepper, washed, de-seeded and coarsely blended
1 carrot, peeled and coarsely blended
1 handful fresh coriander, washed and finely chopped
2 tsp salt
juice of ½ lime
1 tsp coarsely ground black pepper
40g cornflour, sieved
50g rice flour, sieved
2 thick slices of white bread, half-toasted then blended into crumbs
sunflower oil for frying

Crush the chillies and ginger together with a pinch of salt using a pestle and mortar (or a blender), to make a fine masala paste.

Grate the potatoes into a large mixing bowl. Mix in the masala paste and all the remaining ingredients apart from the breadcrumbs and frying oil. Shape into 8 burger patties of approximately 9cm in diameter and 1cm thick. Gently dip each burger in the breadcrumbs.

Heat the frying oil – about 10cm deep – in a large pan over a high heat (or in a deep fat fryer, if you have one) and when you think it is hot enough, test the temperature by dropping a little of the burger mixture into the oil. When it is hot enough, the mixture will quickly spring up to float on the surface. Reduce the heat to medium.

Carefully put a burger in the hot oil and fry for 3 minutes until it turns golden brown and crispy. Remove from the pan using a slotted spoon and place on absorbent kitchen towel. Repeat with the remaining burgers.

Build the burgers to your taste – a seeded bun, lettuce, grated cheese, tomato slices, chilli sauce, ketchup or whatever you like. Serve on their own or with sticky chilli chips (page 225).

SPICY PEA AND POTATO PASTIES (OG, N)

*We Brits love a good pasty and this is my homage to that classic pastry parcel –
with a spicy kick! It uses light and airy puff pastry, which is actually very close to
Indian-style pastry, and it is wrapped around a dense, hearty filling that has a real
warmth of flavour when you bite into it. For a proper take on English pie and
chips, serve with* vagarela beans *(page 136) and/or* masala *chips (page 224).*

SERVES 8

40ml sunflower oil

1 tsp cumin seeds

½ tsp asafetida

10–12 fresh curry leaves, washed

200g frozen petits pois peas,
  thawed

2–4 fresh green chillies (ideally
  Kenyan), finely chopped

2 tsp salt

1 tsp *garam masala*

½ tsp turmeric

4 medium red-skinned (or other
  waxy) potatoes, boiled, peeled and
  cut in 1cm dice

1 handful fresh coriander,
  washed and finely chopped

juice of ¼ lime

8 sheets ready-made all-butter
  puff pastry (38cm x 24cm)

Heat the oil in a thick-based frying pan on a high
heat for 1½ minutes. Reduce the heat to low and
add the cumin seeds, asafetida, curry leaves, peas,
chillies, salt, *garam masala* and turmeric. Stir
everything together, then stir in the cooled diced
potatoes and coriander. Add the lime juice and
cook for 4 minutes. Taste and add seasoning if
required. Remove from the heat and leave to cool
for half an hour.

Lay out the pastry sheets on your worktop and cut
each sheet into 4. Put 3 tablespoonfuls of filling on
one half of a piece of pastry, leaving a gap around
the edge. Fold over the other half of the pastry to
cover the filling completely and seal the edges with
a fork, being careful not to pierce the pastry. Lay on
a large baking tray and repeat with the rest of the
pastry pieces.

Preheat the oven to 240°C/220°C fan/gas mark 9
and bake the pasties for 25 minutes until golden
and crispy.

Serve straight from the oven with *vagarela beans*
(page 136) and/or *masala* chips (page 224).

SPICY VEGGIE PIE (WF, N, HO)

A mashed potato topped pie is one of our favourite British dishes that we've adopted into the Patel kitchen. This version is packed full of fresh, nutritious vegetables and it has just the right combination of spices to ensure that it is flavoursome but not over-powering. We'd love to see more of this sort of thing on proper pub menus.

SERVES 6

Masala
2–4 fresh green chillies (ideally Kenyan), finely chopped
3cm root ginger, peeled
pinch of salt

2 tsp salt
½ tsp coarsely ground black pepper
4 medium red-skinned (or other waxy) potatoes, boiled, peeled and mashed
120g plain live set yoghurt
100g Cheddar cheese, grated
3 carrots, peeled and cut in 1cm dice
130g French beans, topped, tailed and cut in half
50g asparagus, cut in 2cm dice
200g broccoli, cut in 2cm florets
50ml sunflower oil
1 tsp cumin seeds
1 medium onion, cut in 1cm dice
3 large chestnut mushrooms, cut in 1cm slices
1 tsp dried thyme
1 handful fresh coriander, washed and finely chopped
1 jar ready-made béchamel sauce

Crush the chillies and ginger together with a pinch of salt using a pestle and mortar (or a blender), to make a fine masala paste.

Stir a teaspoon of the salt and the black pepper into the mashed potato in a large bowl. Mix through the yoghurt and grated cheese, then set aside.

Put the carrots in a large pan of boiling water on a medium heat and simmer for 2 minutes. Add the French beans, then after 2 minutes the asparagus, then after another 2 minutes the broccoli. Leave everything to boil for 3 minutes, then drain the cooked vegetables and set aside.

Heat the oil in a thick-based frying pan on a high heat for 1½ minutes. Add the cumin seeds and swirl through the oil. Add the onion, stir and cook for 1½ minutes, then add the mushrooms and cook for 1 minute. Take off the heat and stir in the masala paste, thyme, remaining teaspoon of salt and the fresh coriander. Add the vegetables and béchamel sauce and mix everything together before pouring into a baking tray or oven dish (approximately 25cm x 18cm).

Spoon the cheesy mashed potato over the top of the creamy vegetables and bake in a preheated oven at 240°C/220°C fan/gas mark 9 for 30 minutes. Serve with salad and *vagarela* beans (page 136).

INDO-ITALIAN MACARONI CHEESE (N)

Cooking is a real family affair, and whenever my sister, Prabha, came to visit she'd make this macaroni cheese for the children. Even now, whenever her name is mentioned, they talk about her legendary macaroni cheese! It's full of colourful veggies and fresh chillies to get your taste buds tingling.

SERVES 6

85g frozen petits pois peas,
  thawed
1 large carrot, peeled and cut in
  1cm dice
1 medium red-skinned (or other
  waxy) potato, peeled and cut in
  1cm dice
300g macaroni pasta
1 tsp sunflower oil, plus 85ml
1 tsp salt
1 medium onion, cut in 1cm dice
24g butter
1 pepper (or ½ each of two different
  coloured peppers), cut in 1cm dice
55g plain flour, sieved
1 ltr whole milk
4 green chillies (ideally Kenyan),
  finely chopped
2 tsp salt
1¾ tsp coarsely ground black pepper
100g Cheddar cheese, grated,
  to serve

Boil the peas, carrot and potato for 12 minutes, then drain and set aside. Cook the macaroni in boiling water with 1 teaspoon of oil and 1 teaspoon of salt for 10 minutes. Drain and set aside in cold water to prevent further cooking.

Heat 25ml of sunflower oil in a thick-based pan on a medium heat for 30 seconds. Add the onion and cook for 1 minute. Add 8g of the butter and cook the onion uncovered on a low heat for 4 minutes. Tip into a bowl and set aside.

Put another 35ml of sunflower oil and 8g of butter in the pan for 30 seconds. Add the diced pepper and cook on a low heat for 3 minutes, stirring regularly. Tip the pepper into the bowl with the fried onion.

Heat the remaining 25ml of sunflower oil in the same pan for 20 seconds on medium. Mix the flour into the hot oil and gently stir for 1 minute before adding the final 8g of butter. Continue stirring and breaking up the doughy mixture for a further 3 minutes. Take off the heat and gently pour one third of the milk into the pan. Place back on the heat and stir for 3 minutes, or until you have a smooth, creamy texture. Add the remaining milk and keep cooking and stirring for 3 minutes.

Now tip the peas, carrot, potato, macaroni, onion, pepper and fresh green chillies into the white sauce, season with the salt and pepper and cook for a final 2 minutes, still stirring.

Serve in wide bowls, topped with grated cheese and a generous seasoning of salt and ground black pepper with sticky chilli chips (page 225).

INDO-ITALIAN VEGGIE LASAGNE (N)

Lasagne is another favourite classic Italian dish loved by all the Patel family, but we can't do without our dose of green chillies and fresh coriander. This is a quick-and-easy recipe, using tinned tomatoes and ready-made béchamel sauce. Traditional Italian vegetables that you'd expect to see in any good veggie lasagne – such as aubergine, courgette and pepper – are perfect for soaking up the spices, ensuring the taste of India is infused throughout.

SERVES 4

Masala
4–6 fresh green chillies (ideally Kenyan)
4–6 cloves of garlic, soaked and peeled
pinch of salt

Vegetable sauce
50ml sunflower oil
1 medium onion, cut in 1cm dice
1 red pepper, cut in 1cm dice
½ large aubergine, cut in 1cm dice
1 medium courgette, quartered and cut in ½cm dice
8 chestnut mushrooms, cut in 1cm slices
2 tsp salt
1 handful fresh coriander, washed and finely chopped
½ tsp coarsely ground black pepper
pinch of turmeric
2 tsp dried Italian mixed herbs
1 x 400g tin peeled plum tomatoes, blended

8 lasagne sheets
1 jar ready-made béchamel sauce
200g Cheddar cheese, grated
½ large aubergine, thinly sliced
3 cherry tomatoes, thinly sliced

Crush the chillies and garlic with a pinch of salt using a pestle and mortar (or blender), to make a fine masala paste.

Heat the oil in a large thick-based pan on a high heat for 2 minutes, then add the onion and fry for 2 minutes. Stirring regularly, add the pepper and fry for 2 minutes, then the aubergine (fry for 1½ minutes), then the courgette (1½ minutes), then the mushrooms (1½ minutes). Reduce the heat to low and stir in the masala paste, salt, fresh coriander, black pepper, turmeric and 1 teaspoon of the dried Italian herbs. After 1½ minutes, turn the heat back up to high, stir well and add the tinned tomatoes. Leave the sauce to cook for 1 minute before reducing the heat to medium. Cover and cook for 5 minutes before removing from the heat.

Soak the lasagne sheets in boiling water in a large, deep pan for 3 minutes, being careful that they don't overlap and stick together.

Spread a layer of the vegetable sauce about ½cm thick in the base of a deep baking dish (about 24cm x 16cm). Cover with a layer of lasagne sheets, breaking them in pieces to fill all the gaps. Pour one third of the béchamel sauce on top and spread evenly. Now sprinkle 70g of the cheese over the béchamel. Repeat this process to create another level of sauce-pasta-béchamel-cheese layers.

Repeat for a third time, but finish with the last of the béchamel sauce (don't put the last of the cheese on yet). Lay the sliced aubergine and cherry tomatoes over the béchamel, then sprinkle with the remaining cheese and Italian herbs.

Bake in a preheated oven at 240°C/220°C fan/gas mark 9 for 30 minutes. Serve generous portions, piping hot, with a fresh salad alongside.

INDO-ITALIAN VEGGIE CANNELLONI (N)

Indian spices and Italian herbs both have strong flavour profiles, which means they can stand up to one another well, and a tomato sauce is the perfect backdrop for them. This dish is relatively new to me, but it's already a favourite – not least because using pre-made sauces means it's ready in half the time. I don't usually use jarred sauces, but the additional flavourings I add give them extra depth and warmth, and I think sometimes it's good to take a few shortcuts. I use ricotta rather than Indian paneer cheese here, because the consistency is much better for this dish.

SERVES 4

Masala
3–5 green chillies (ideally Kenyan)
4–6 cloves of garlic, soaked and
  peeled
pinch of salt

2 tsp sunflower oil, plus 50ml
½ tsp salt, plus 2 tsp
20 dried cannelloni pasta tubes
1½ tsp cumin seeds
1 medium onion, cut in 1cm dice
4 large chestnut mushrooms, cut in
  1cm slices
½ tsp coarsely ground black pepper
1 handful fresh coriander,
  washed and finely chopped
1 tsp rosemary
1 tsp sage
250g spinach, washed and chopped
120g ricotta cheese
500g jar ready-made Italian
  tomato sauce
500g jar ready-made béchamel sauce
½ tsp dried Italian mixed herbs

Crush the chillies and garlic together with a pinch of salt using a pestle and mortar (or a blender), to make a fine masala paste.

Put 2 teaspoons of oil and ½ teaspoon of salt in 2 litres of boiling water over a high heat. Once simmering, add the cannelloni, cover and cook for 3½ minutes. Drain and set aside in cold water to prevent further cooking.

Heat the 50ml of sunflower oil in a thick-based frying pan on a high heat for 1½ minutes. Add the cumin seeds and swirl in the oil, then stir in the onions and fry for 2 minutes. Stir in the chestnut mushrooms and fry for 2 minutes. Reduce the heat to medium and continue cooking for 30 seconds, then stir in the masala paste, 2 teaspoons of salt, black pepper, fresh coriander, the rosemary and half the sage. Cook for a minute before stirring in the spinach. Cook for 30 seconds, then take off the heat and stir the ricotta through gently.

Cover the bottom of a baking tray or oven dish with the tomato sauce. Carefully fill the pasta tubes with the filling mixture and place on top of the tomato base. Cover the cannelloni with the béchamel sauce and sprinkle with the remaining sage and the Italian herbs. Bake in a preheated oven at 240°C/220°C fan/gas mark 9 for 30 minutes.

Serve large portions, steaming hot, with salad alongside.

PANEER RAVIOLI

These delicate ravioli are Indo-Italian fusion at its absolute best. It may seem like quite a jump from my usual style of cooking, but small bites, such as steamed dumplings and bhajis, are very popular in Gujarati cooking and these little pasta parcels are quite similar in many ways. I owe thanks to my super-talented daughter-in-law, Minal, for inspiring me to experiment with these. The soft paneer filling is given some 'bite' with coarsely ground nuts, and the tomato sauce is infused with rich, warm spices. It's a very delicate dish with wonderful layers of flavour – perfect for a special occasion, as it does take a little while to make the pasta by hand.

SERVES 4

Dough
300g '00' flour, sieved
1 tsp salt
25ml sunflower oil
120ml warm water

Filling
185g *paneer* cheese, grated
15g cashew nuts, coarsely ground
15g almonds, coarsely ground
15g pistachios, coarsely ground
90g double cream
30g sugar

Sauce
85ml sunflower oil
2 tsp cumin seeds
3 cloves
6 whole peppercorns
8 cloves of garlic, soaked, peeled
   and halved
5 large vine tomatoes, cut in
   1cm slices
3cm root ginger, peeled and blended
1 tsp turmeric
2 tsp salt
2 tsp ground coriander

Mix the flour and salt for the ravioli together on a clean work surface or flat tray. Make a well in the middle of the flour and pour in the oil. Gently mix the oil through the flour before gradually adding the water whilst mixing and kneading the dough. Cover the tight, firm dough with clingfilm and leave to rest for 10–15 minutes at room temperature.

Mix the filling ingredients together in a large bowl and set aside.

Heat 70ml of the oil for the sauce in a thick-based frying pan on a high heat for 1½ minutes. Add the cumin seeds, cloves, peppercorns and garlic, swirl through the oil and fry on a medium heat for 30 seconds. Add the tomatoes, increase the heat to high and let them sizzle for a minute before stirring. Cook covered for 4 minutes, stirring halfway through. Take off the heat and use a blender to blitz to a smooth texture (I do this with a stick blender in a jug).

Wash and dry the frying pan, then pour in the remaining 15ml of oil and place on a high heat. Add the ginger and fry for 15 seconds before pouring in the tomato mixture. Add the turmeric, salt, ground coriander, ground cumin, chilli powder, *garam masala* and fresh coriander and cook for 1 minute. Turn to low heat, cover and simmer for 12 minutes before removing from the heat.

CONTINUED OVERLEAF

2 tsp ground cumin

½ tsp medium red chilli powder

1 tsp *garam masala*

1 handful fresh coriander, washed and finely chopped

2 tsp sunflower oil, for the pasta water

½ tsp salt, for the pasta water

Now divide the ravioli dough into 40 pieces (each about 12g) and use a rolling pin to roll each one into a 7cm-diameter disc. Place 10–12g of filling in the middle of a piece of dough, then place another piece on top and nip the edges together. Make sure the ravioli is properly sealed by pressing the edges down with a fork, being careful not to pierce it. Repeat until all the ravioli are stuffed and sealed. Lay them on a tray and cover with a tea towel so that they don't dry out.

Put the oil and salt for cooking the pasta in 3 litres of boiling water in a large thick-based pan. Turn the heat to high and carefully drop the ravioli parcels into the boiling water. Cook uncovered for 6 minutes, then drain and rinse in cold water.

Bring the sauce back to a simmer and add the ravioli, stirring gently for 2 minutes. Serve piping hot in large, wide bowls, with a green salad and maybe some garlic bread.

SPICY MUSHROOM AND PEPPER PIZZA (N)

Breads are very important in Indian cooking, but rather than using them to scoop up your food, here masses of tasty veggies are piled on top of a doughy base in my take on the classic pizza. It's very filling – your eyes might tell you that you need three pieces, but one or two is usually plenty. If you have any leftovers, they taste great the next day too, once the flavours have had extra time to infuse. This is the dish I serve up if anyone fancies a change from curry in the Patel house – which does occasionally happen!

SERVES 4

Dough
450g strong white fine flour, sieved
7g fast-acting yeast
1 tsp salt
1¼ tsp sugar
2 tsp coarse ground black pepper
25ml sunflower oil
300ml lukewarm water

Masala
2–3 green chillies (ideally Kenyan)
3–5 cloves of garlic, soaked and
  peeled
pinch of salt

Sauce
50ml sunflower oil
½ medium onion, cut in 1½cm dice
½ red pepper, cut in 1½cm dice
1 x 400g tin peeled plum tomatoes,
  blended
¾ tsp salt
60g tomato ketchup

Mix the flour and yeast together in a large bowl before adding the salt, sugar, pepper and oil. Using your fingers, work the oil and seasoning into the flour. Add 200ml of water and bring everything together, working it with your hands before adding the remaining water and then kneading, stretching and folding the dough on the worktop until you've worked all the sticky dough off your hands.

Lightly oil your hands, knead the dough shape into a large ball and seal in a large container. Leave to prove somewhere warm, like the airing cupboard, for 4–5 hours.

Crush the chillies and garlic together with a pinch of salt using a pestle and mortar (or a blender), to make a fine masala paste.

Heat the oil for the sauce in a large thick-based pan for 1 minute. Add the onion and pepper and stir for 7 minutes until slightly brown. Add the masala paste and stir through for 30 seconds to infuse. Gently stir in the blended tomatoes and salt and simmer uncovered for 7 minutes, stirring occasionally, until the sauce is thick and full of flavour. Stir in the ketchup, remove from the heat and set aside.

Preheat the oven to 240°C/220°C fan/gas mark 9. If possible, set the shelves 12cm apart from each other and from the top/bottom of the oven. Coat your

Topping

310g mature Cheddar cheese,
 grated
10 spring onions, cut in 1cm dice
1 red pepper, cut in 1cm dice
1 green pepper, cut in 1cm dice
6 chestnut mushrooms, cut in
 ½cm dice
½ medium onion, cut in 1½cm dice
2 large vine tomatoes, cut in
 1cm slices
2 jalapeño peppers, cut in ½cm dice

worktop and a rolling pin with some oil. Divide
the dough in half and roll each piece into a roughly
25cm disc. Lay each pizza base on a perforated
pizza pan or an oil-lined baking tray and push the
dough out towards the edges using your fingers
until each base is roughly 30cm in diameter. Bake
the bases for 5 minutes.

Carefully remove the trays from the oven and
spread the sauce generously over the pizza bases.
Gently scatter half the cheese over each base. Mix
all the topping vegetables apart from the tomatoes
and jalapeños in a large bowl and divide two-thirds
of the mixture between the two pizzas, scattering
the veggies around to ensure that each slice will have
a good selection. Then spread the remaining cheese
over the pizzas. Divide the final third of the topping
vegetables between the two pizzas and scatter evenly
over them. Finally, gently place the tomatoes and
jalapeños evenly on top.

Place the trays back in the oven and bake for 25
minutes. Leave to rest for 5 minutes before cutting
into slices and serving – it needs no accompaniment.

CHILLI PANEER ⟨ Indo-Chinese marinated cheese stir-fry

(N, HO)

Paneer is fantastic in a stir-fry because of its combination of crisp and creamy textures, perfect alongside the crunchy fresh vegetables. This street food classic will quickly become one of those recipes you make all the time, as it's just so easy and delicious.

SERVES 4

sunflower oil for deep-frying the
  paneer, plus 70ml for stir-frying
350g *paneer* cheese, cut in 1½cm
  dice
4cm root ginger, peeled and finely
  chopped
6–8 cloves of garlic, soaked,
  peeled and finely chopped
6–8 fresh green chillies (ideally
  Kenyan), finely chopped
2 large onions, cut in ½cm slices
2 red peppers, cut in ½cm slices
2 tsp dark soy sauce
½ tsp hot red chilli sauce
½ tsp green chilli sauce
2 tsp salt
½ tsp coarsely ground black pepper
2½ tsp malt vinegar
2 handfuls fresh coriander,
  washed and finely chopped
3 spring onions, finely sliced

Heat the oil – about 10cm deep – in a large pan over a high heat (or in a deep fat fryer, if you have one) and when you think it is hot enough, test the temperature by dropping a piece of *paneer* into the oil. If it is up to temperature, it will bubble vigorously. Add the rest of the *paneer* and reduce the heat to medium. Gently stir for 1 minute with a wooden or heatproof plastic spoon, separating the *paneer* pieces if they stick together, then remove from the oil and place straight into cold water to rinse away any excess oil. After a few minutes, take the *paneer* out of the water and place on absorbent kitchen towel for 15 minutes.

Heat 70ml of oil in a large wok (or large, deep frying pan) on a medium heat for 1 minute, swirling it around the pan. Stir-fry the ginger and garlic for 2 minutes, then stir in the chillies and fry for 20 seconds, keeping them in the bottom of the pan. Add the onions and stir-fry for 1½ minutes, then add the peppers and fry, stirring occasionally, for 2½ minutes. Finally, add the *paneer*, soy sauce, red and green chilli sauces, salt, pepper, vinegar and 1 handful of the fresh coriander and stir-fry for 3 minutes.

Serve straight from the wok in large bowls, garnished with the rest of the fresh coriander and the spring onions.

CHINESE BHEL ⟨ Indo-Chinese street-style rice and noodles
(V, N)

When made on the streets in India, this dish is action-packed and theatrical. The street chef will have all his ingredients prepared, ready to throw into the pan and show off his skills. With the arrival of fast food chains, it's sad to see some of the street food vendors disappear, but I think this dish will be around for a while yet.

SERVES 4

Rice
125g rice (ideally Tilda basmati)
2 tsp sunflower oil
½ tsp salt

Masala
3 fresh green chillies (ideally Kenyan)
3 cloves of garlic, soaked and peeled
2cm root ginger, peeled
pinch of salt

Dough balls
100g plain flour, sieved
50g cornflour, sieved
½ carrot, peeled and coarsely blended
¼ yellow pepper, coarsely blended
100g white cabbage, washed and
  blended
1 tsp salt
1½ tsp dark soy sauce
1 tsp malt vinegar
small pinch coarsely ground black
  pepper
¼ handful fresh coriander, washed
  and finely chopped
15ml sunflower oil, plus more for
  deep-frying
35ml water

Rinse the rice and drain immediately. Place in a large thick-based pan on a high heat with 150ml of water, 2 teaspoons of sunflower oil and ½ teaspoon of salt. The oil will help to ensure that the water doesn't boil over. Once the water has come to the boil, gently stir and reduce the heat to medium. Simmer uncovered for 12 minutes, then cover and cook for a further 8 minutes. Check that the rice is cooked and set aside. It should be quite sticky, unlike the fluffy rice you would serve with curry.

Crush the chillies, garlic and ginger together with a pinch of salt using a pestle and mortar (or a blender), to make a fine masala paste.

Mix the flours in a large bowl and add the blended vegetables, masala paste, salt, soy sauce, vinegar, black pepper, fresh coriander and 15ml of sunflower oil. Mix everything through using your fingers and thumbs, and allow the flavours to infuse into the dough. Add the water and keep mixing until you have a sticky, gooey dough. Lightly oil your hands and make the dough into 3cm-diameter balls (about 18). Don't compress them too much – keep some air to ensure they are light. Scrape any excess dough from your hands in between rolling and re-oil them as necessary.

Heat the frying oil – about 10cm deep – in a large pan over a high heat (or in a deep fat fryer, if you have one) and when you think it is hot enough, test the temperature by dropping a little of the dough into the oil. When it is up to temperature, the mixture will quickly spring back up to float on the surface. Reduce the heat to medium.

CONTINUED OVERLEAF

Noodles
15ml sunflower oil
2 nests (approx. 100g) dried
  wholewheat egg-free noodles
½ tsp salt

Stir-fry
75ml sunflower oil
4cm root ginger, peeled and finely
  chopped
4–6 cloves of garlic, soaked, peeled
  and finely chopped
4–8 fresh green chillies (ideally
  Kenyan), finely chopped
1 carrot, peeled and cut in ½cm
  strips
1 medium onion, cut in ½cm strips
½ red pepper, cut in ½cm strips
200g white cabbage, cut in ½cm
  strips
2 tsp dark soy sauce
2 tsp salt
1 tsp pepper
3 tsp malt vinegar
1 handful fresh coriander,
  washed and finely chopped
40g spring onion, finely sliced

Place a few balls at a time in the hot oil and fry for 6 minutes. Remove them from the oil with a slotted spoon and place on absorbent kitchen towel. Repeat with the remaining balls, making sure you let the oil come back up to full heat in between batches.

Bring 1 litre of water to the boil in a large pan and add 15ml of oil. Break the noodle nests in half over the water and gently drop them in. Stir, add the salt and cook for 3½ minutes. Drain, rinse with cold water to stop them cooking any further and set aside.

Now, to bring everything together, heat a large wok on a high heat for 30 seconds, then turn down to medium. Swirl the oil around the bottom of the wok for 30 seconds, then add the chopped ginger, garlic and chillies and fry for 1 minute, allowing the fresh flavours to infuse. Add the carrot, increase the heat to high and fry for 1 minute, then add the onion and stir-fry for 1 minute, followed by the pepper for another minute. Keep stirring and tossing the vegetables through the oil. Add the cabbage, mix through and reduce the heat to low. Stir in the soy sauce, salt, pepper, vinegar and half the fresh coriander and mix well.

Turn the heat back up to medium. Gently loosen the rice from its pan and add to the wok, gradually breaking it up. Tip in the drained noodles and dough balls, then mix everything together (I use two long-handled spoons or forks). Make sure you really lift all the ingredients through each other to combine and bring out the flavours.

Serve immediately in large bowls, and garnish with spring onions and the remaining fresh coriander.

HAKKA NOODLES ⟨ Indo-Chinese street food noodles

(V, N, HO)

Minal learned to cook this when she was growing up in India, dreaming of one day becoming a chef. It is a particularly popular street food dish that you can easily make at home. The secret lies in ensuring that the colourful vegetables retain some crunch, whilst giving them enough time to infuse in all the spices. You can have some fun pretending to be a performer on the streets of India and tossing the ingredients as high as you dare while you fry.

SERVES 4

70ml sunflower oil

6–8 cloves of garlic, peeled and
  finely chopped

4cm root ginger, peeled and finely
  chopped

2–4 green chillies (ideally Kenyan),
  finely chopped

½ medium onion, cut in ½cm slices

2 carrots, peeled and cut into
  ½cm strips

90g broccoli, cut in 1cm slices

3 large asparagus spears, cut in
  ½cm slices

½ green pepper, cut in ½cm slices

100g white cabbage, cut in 2cm
  slices

6–8 chestnut mushrooms, cut in
  ½cm slices

160g fresh noodles

2 tsp dark soy sauce

½ tsp green chilli sauce

½ tsp hot red chilli sauce

½ tsp coarsely ground black pepper

2 tsp salt

3 tsp malt vinegar

2 handfuls fresh coriander,
  washed and finely chopped

3 spring onions, finely sliced

Heat the oil in a large wok on a high heat for 45 seconds. Reduce the heat to medium, add the garlic and ginger and fry for 1 minute. Turn the heat back up to high, add the chillies and fry for 1 minute. Stirring all the time, add the onion (fry for 1 minute), then the carrots (fry for 1 minute), then the broccoli (30 seconds), asparagus (40 seconds), pepper (30 seconds,) and cabbage (40 seconds), then finally the mushrooms (toss and cook for 1 minute).

Now add the noodles, soy sauce, red and green chilli sauces, pepper, salt, vinegar and 1 handful of the fresh coriander. Reduce the heat to low and stir-fry for 2 minutes, folding in the noodles and making sure that the vegetables and spices are evenly mixed through.

Serve piping hot, straight from the wok, in large bowls garnished with the remaining fresh coriander and the spring onions.

SZECHUAN RICE ⟨ Indo-Chinese fried rice

(V, N, HO)

Chinese communities have lived in India for more than a hundred years, and Chinese cuisine now plays a huge role in Indian cooking. This Indo-Chinese street food classic features a staple Patel family ingredient, rice, so it's both familiar and foreign to us. It fuses the flavours of India and China perfectly to give the fresh, crunchy vegetables a real kick.

SERVES 4

250g rice (ideally Tilda basmati), soaked in cold water for 30 minutes, then drained

2 tsp sunflower oil, plus 55ml for stir-frying

½ tsp salt, plus 1 tsp

60g frozen petits pois peas, thawed

60g French beans, topped, tailed and cut in 2cm dice

½ yellow pepper, cut in ½cm slices

55g broccoli, cut into small, halved florets

3 large asparagus spears, cut in ½ cm dice

2 carrots, peeled and cut in 1cm dice

2–4 cloves of garlic, peeled and finely chopped

3cm root ginger, peeled and finely chopped

1–3 green chillies (ideally Kenyan), finely chopped

40g tomato ketchup

2 handfuls fresh coriander, washed and finely chopped

2 tsp malt vinegar

½ tsp coarsely ground black pepper

1 tsp dark soy sauce

½ tsp hot red chilli sauce

½ tsp green chilli sauce

3 spring onions, finely sliced

Put the drained rice in a large thick-based pan on a high heat with 300ml of boiling water, 2 teaspoons of sunflower oil and half a teaspoon of salt, and cook for 4 minutes (the oil will help to ensure that the water doesn't boil over). Stir, add another 100ml of boiling water, cook for a minute, then reduce the heat to low. Cook covered for 5 minutes, then take off the heat. Check that the rice is cooked, then leave to rest covered until you are ready to add it to the wok.

Simmer the peas, French beans, pepper, broccoli, asparagus and carrots in 1 litre of water in a large pan on full heat for 3 minutes. Drain the vegetables and dunk in cold water for 30 seconds (to stop them cooking any further), then drain again and set aside.

Heat 30ml of the sunflower oil in a large wok on a high heat for 45 seconds. Reduce the heat to medium, add the garlic and ginger and fry for 1 minute. Turn the heat back up to high, add the chillies and fry for 30 seconds. Turn off the heat and mix in the ketchup, 1 handful of fresh coriander, plus the vinegar, pepper, salt, soy sauce and red and green chilli sauces. Pour into a bowl and set aside, then thoroughly wash and dry the wok.

Heat the remaining 25ml sunflower oil in the wok on a medium heat for 30 seconds. Add the drained vegetables and stir through the oil for 1½ minutes. Add the remaining fresh coriander, the spring onions and the sauce that you set aside in a bowl and stir-fry for 45 seconds. Break up the rice (if it has clumped together), mix it in and stir-fry everything together for 2 minutes, ensuring that the vegetables and sauce are well mixed into the rice.

Serve piping hot, fresh from the wok, in large bowls.

MANCHURIAN CABBAGE DOUGH BALLS WITH VEGETABLE STIR-FRY (V, N)

Living in a rural village, we were always hungry for new ideas to inspire our cooking. My dad used to travel to the city once a week for study, and he'd often bring back unusual vegetables from the markets there, or he'd tell us about dishes he'd eaten or seen being made on the street. This is a version of one of those classic Indo-Chinese street food dishes he told us about.

SERVES 5

Masala
6–8 fresh green chillies (ideally Kenyan)
5–7 cloves of garlic, soaked and peeled
5cm root ginger, peeled
pinch of salt

Dough balls
240g plain flour, sieved
130g cornflour, sieved
1 carrot, peeled and coarsely blended
½ green pepper, coarsely blended
225g white cabbage, washed and blended
2½ tsp salt
3 tsp dark soy sauce
2 tsp malt vinegar
½ tsp coarsely ground black pepper
½ handful fresh coriander, washed and finely chopped
30ml sunflower, plus more for deep-frying
75ml water

Stir-fry
50ml sunflower oil
4–5 cloves of garlic, soaked, peeled and finely chopped
5cm root ginger, peeled and finely chopped
2–4 fresh green chillies (ideally Kenyan), finely chopped

Crush the chillies, garlic and ginger together with a pinch of salt using a pestle and mortar (or a blender), to make a fine masala paste.

Mix the flours in a large bowl and add the blended vegetables, masala paste, salt, soy sauce, vinegar, black pepper, fresh coriander and oil. Mix everything through using your fingers and thumbs, and allow all the flavours to infuse into the dough. Add the water and keep mixing until you have a sticky, gooey dough.

Lightly oil your hands and make the dough into 3cm-diameter balls (it should yield at least 30). Don't compress them too much – keep some air to ensure they are light. Scrape any excess dough from your hands in between rolling and re-oil them as necessary.

Heat the frying oil – about 10cm deep – in a large pan over a high heat (or in a deep fat fryer, if you have one) and when you think it is hot enough, test the temperature by dropping a little of the dough into the oil. When it is up to temperature, the mixture will quickly spring back up to float on the surface. Reduce the heat to medium.

Place a few balls at a time in the hot oil and fry for 6 minutes. Remove them from the oil with a slotted spoon and place on absorbent kitchen towel. Repeat with the remaining balls, making sure you let the oil come back up to full heat in between batches.

Heat the oil in a large wok on a high heat for 45 seconds, then turn down to medium. Add the garlic and ginger and fry for 1 minute. Turn the heat

½ carrot, peeled and cut into ½cm
   strips
½ red pepper, cut in ½cm strips
185g white cabbage, cut in ½cm
   strips
2 tsp dark soy sauce
1½ tsp salt
½ tsp pepper
2 tsp malt vinegar
1 handful fresh coriander, washed
   and finely chopped
15g cornflour, diluted in 400ml
   water
40g spring onion, finely chopped
   into discs

back up to high, add the chillies and fry for
30 seconds, then add the carrot (stir-fry for 2
minutes) and the pepper (30 seconds). Finally add
the cabbage, toss all the vegetables through the oil
and fry for a further 4 minutes.

Turn the heat back down to low and add the dough
balls, soy sauce, salt, pepper, vinegar and half the
fresh coriander. Stir through and cook for 1½ minutes. Add the diluted cornflour (making sure you
don't leave any behind), stir in and cook on full heat
for 2 minutes.

Serve immediately on a bed of fluffy *baath* rice (page
213), garnished with the remaining fresh coriander
and the spring onions.

MANCHOW SOUP ᐸ hot and spicy stir-fry soup

(v, og, n, ho)

This fiery, healthy Indo-Chinese soup is both comforting and revitalising. The crunchy vegetables give it some real bite and it's ready in minutes. It's also great for soothing a stuffy nose.

SERVES 4

25ml sunflower oil

2cm root ginger, peeled and finely chopped

3–4 cloves of garlic, peeled and finely chopped

2 fresh green chillies (ideally Kenyan), finely chopped

2 medium carrots, peeled and cut in ½cm dice

50g French beans, topped, tailed and cut in ½cm dice

140g white cabbage, cut in ½cm dice

1 yellow pepper, cut in ½cm dice

2 tsp dark soy sauce

¼ tsp green chilli sauce

¼ tsp hot red chilli sauce

2 tsp malt vinegar

2 tsp salt

¼ tsp coarsely ground black pepper

1.2 ltr boiling water

2 tsp cornflour, diluted in 50ml water

1 handful fresh coriander, washed and finely chopped

2 spring onions, finely chopped

Heat the oil in a large wok on a medium heat for 40 seconds. Add the ginger and garlic and fry for 40 seconds. Increase the heat to high, add the chillies and mix through the oil for 30 seconds to infuse all the flavours. Add the carrots and stir-fry for 1 minute, then the French beans (stir-fry for 1 minute), then the cabbage (1½ minutes) and the pepper (1½ minutes). Reduce the heat to low.

Stir through the soy sauce, green and red chilli sauces, vinegar, salt and pepper, then tip the contents of the wok into a large, thick-based pan containing the boiling water and diluted cornflour. Cook uncovered on a high heat for 5 minutes.

Serve the soup immediately in large, deep bowls, garnished with the fresh coriander and spring onions.

INDO-MEXICAN VEGGIE ENCHILADAS

Mexican food is interesting to me as a chef because of the way it happily combines chillies, vegetables and cheese – beans feature a lot too, and are very popular in Gujarati cooking. Enchiladas are real classic Mexican fare, but I have given them a slight twist of my own (of course!), using carom seeds to infuse the vegetables. I find that carom works particularly well with mild-flavoured vegetables like courgettes. My version is hot and spicy, like the original, but also has an additional warmth.

SERVES 4

Masala
2–4 fresh green chillies
 (ideally Kenyan)
1–2 cloves of garlic, soaked
 and peeled
4cm root ginger, peeled
pinch of salt

30ml sunflower oil
1 tsp carom seeds
½ courgette, cut in ½cm slices
5 chestnut mushrooms, cut in
 ½cm slices
3 spring onions, finely chopped
1½ tsp salt
½ tsp coarsely ground black pepper
2 tsp Mexican seasoning
2 handfuls fresh coriander,
 washed and finely chopped
1 x 400g tin black beans, rinsed
 and drained (drained weight 240g)
1 x 300g tin mixed beans, rinsed
 and drained (drained weight 180g)
8 soft cornflour tortillas (18cm
 diameter)
500g ready-made tomato sauce
100g Cheddar cheese, grated

Crush the chillies and garlic together with a pinch of salt using a pestle and mortar (or a blender), to make a fine masala paste.

Heat the oil in a thick-based frying pan on a medium heat for 1½ minutes. Add the carom seeds and swirl into the oil for 10 seconds. Add the courgettes and stir through for 45 seconds, then add the mushrooms and stir-fry for 1 minute, then tip in the spring onions and stir-fry for 45 seconds. Reduce the heat to low and stir in the masala paste, salt, pepper, 1 teaspoon of the Mexican seasoning and 1 handful of the fresh coriander. Stir in the beans and cook for 1½ minutes before removing from the heat.

Heat each tortilla in a dry frying pan for 6 seconds, then spoon on one-eighth of the spice-infused vegetable and bean mix. Roll the tortilla up and lay it, seam-side down, in a large baking tray or oven dish. Repeat with the other tortillas. Pour the tomato sauce over the top of the filled tortillas, then sprinkle on the other teaspoon of the Mexican seasoning and the grated cheese. Bake in a preheated oven at 220°C/200°C fan/gas mark 7 for 20 minutes.

Serve piping hot, with a leafy salad and coleslaw.

CHANA DHAL VADA · Indian-style 'falafel' in toasted pitta

(N)

Most cuisines around the world share some familiar ways of preparing food,
but making use of their own local ingredients. This Greek-inspired dish uses
classic Gujarati spices to produce gorgeous, crisp, spicy 'falafel', which are then
stuffed into pitta with cumin-infused sour cream and imli *chutney (page 241).*
We enjoy tucking into these as a change from the breads and bhajis we're used to.

SERVES 4

Masala
2–4 fresh green chillies (ideally
  Kenyan)
1–2 cloves of garlic, soaked and
  peeled
4cm root ginger, peeled
pinch of salt

50g *chana dhal*
50g coarse gram (chickpea) flour,
  sieved
550ml warm water
1¼ tsp salt
½ tsp sugar
pinch of turmeric
sunflower oil for deep-frying
2 tsp cumin seeds
300ml sour cream
6–8 pitta breads
½ iceberg lettuce
1 handful mixed leaf salad
1 vine tomato, sliced
1 medium onion, sliced
200ml *imli* chutney (page 241)
1 handful fresh coriander,
  washed and finely chopped

Put the *chana dhal* in 500ml of warm water, and
the gram flour in 50ml of warm water, cover and
leave to soak at room temperature overnight.

Crush the chillies, garlic and ginger together with
a pinch of salt using a pestle and mortar (or a
blender), to make a fine masala paste.

Drain the *chana dhal* and blend to a fine texture in
a blender. Tip into a bowl and combine with the
masala paste, gram flour (which will have soaked up
its water), salt, sugar and turmeric to make a paste.

Heat the frying oil – about 10cm deep – in a large
pan over a high heat (or in a deep fat fryer, if you
have one) and when you think it is hot enough, test
the temperature by dropping a little of the paste into
the oil. When it is up to temperature, the mixture
will quickly spring back up to float on the surface.
Reduce the heat to medium.

Taking 1 tablespoonful of the paste at a time,
carefully drop into the hot oil using your hand or
with a spoon. The mixture should yield around
18 *vada*. Fry as many pieces as will fit in the pan for
4–5 minutes, then carefully remove with a slotted
spoon and place on absorbent kitchen towel to cool.
Repeat with the remaining mixture, making sure
you let the oil come back up to full heat in
between batches.

Toast the cumin seeds in a dry frying pan for
30 seconds. Swirl around the pan, then toast for

another 30 seconds before removing from the heat. Crush the toasted seeds with a rolling pin or pestle and mortar, then mix into the sour cream.

Lightly warm the pittas in a toaster, then cut them open to make a pocket. Line the thickest side with a good dollop of the sour cream and layer up the iceberg, mixed leaf salad, tomato and onion. Drizzle with some of the *imli* chutney, then stuff with 3–4 cooled *vada*. Add a final dollop of sour cream and garnish with some fresh coriander. Serve as a filling, satisfying snack or light meal.

SAFFRON & GINGER PANNA COTTA (WE, OG, N)

*Like most Indian desserts, this classic Italian pudding is creamy and sweet:
perfect for infusing with aromatic spices. The luxuriously smooth milky jelly
is flavoured with saffron and ginger, making a truly exquisite dish.
You'll need six 150ml moulds – you can use individual pudding moulds,
darioles, ramekins or even heatproof teacups.*

SERVES 6

3cm root ginger, peeled and grated
½ tsp saffron
420ml milk
200ml double cream
2g agar agar
6 tsp sugar

Take the grated ginger and wrap it in a piece of muslin. Squeeze through the cloth until you have 1 teaspoon of juice, then discard the pulp.

Soak half the saffron in 50ml of the milk for 5 minutes. Add it to a pan containing the rest of the milk, the cream, the agar agar and the sugar. Cook on a medium heat, stirring until the agar agar and sugar are dissolved, then gently simmer for 4½ minutes, being careful not to let it burn. Stir in the ginger juice and simmer for a further 2 minutes.

Divide the mixture equally between the pudding moulds and sprinkle with the rest of the saffron so that you can see the bright orange streaks floating in the liquid. Leave to cool and set, then place in the fridge until you are ready to serve.

Soak the moulds in boiling water for 30–60 seconds, then roll the moulds between the palms of your hands to loosen the panna cotta from the sides. Tip onto individual plates with some fresh berries or chopped fruit.

FEASTS
FESTIVITIES
AND SWEETS

CHAKRI STRIPS ‹ crispy rice and potato snacks

BATAKA CHEVDA ‹ Kaushy's Bombay mix

CHORA FARI ‹ spicy 'poppadom' crisps

KAKADHIA ‹ crisp sugar biscuits

BHAKAR VADI ‹ sweet and tangy fried rolls

UNDHIYU ‹ classic Gujarati mixed vegetable pot

VEGETABLE KOFTA ‹ vegetable patties in coriander,
garlic and tomato sauce

DHAL BHATI & CHURMA ‹ lentil soup with sweet and
savoury dumplings

DUM BIRYANI ‹ layered vegetable rice

HYDERABADI BIRYANI ‹ rich vegetable rice with
mint masala

GOOGRA ‹ spiced nut parcels

INDIAN FRUIT SALAD

ANGUR RABRI ‹ creamy milk pudding

SEV ‹ sweet cardamom vermicelli

We Indians love a celebration! There are so many feast days in our religious calendar that we're never far away from a party of some kind or other. At festivals there might be fireworks and music and dancing, but, of course, there will always be lots of delicious food too. There's a kite festival that I remember vividly as a child. Everyone made their own kite and then we'd go out into the fields or climb on top of the house to fly them; there'd be hundreds of different-coloured kites in the air, all with their decorative tails dancing in the wind below. Afterwards, we'd rush back inside and eat a warming stew made from lots of seasonal ingredients.

As you know, I love food to be a bit of an occasion – both the making and eating of it – and so cooking for a festival brings me real pleasure. I'd happily prepare a festival feast almost every day, but sadly there just isn't the time – and I'm sure it wouldn't be very good for our waistlines either!

When Heston Blumenthal was filming his television series *Great British Food*, he came to Bradford – the curry capital of Britain. The team at Prashad, along with my sons Bobby and Mayur, had the pleasure of cooking with him. Like us Gujaratis, Heston makes eating a real event and his meals often involve a lot of ceremony. This chapter is about how you can recreate this type of culinary experience at home with feasts and sweets to wow your guests. There is a certain element of showing off here, and the way you present these is almost as important as the taste.

My husband, Mohan, and I have catered for many huge celebrations and we really love this type of cooking and eating. When we ran our small deli in Bradford, our favourite time of year was Diwali, when we would prepare up to 150 kilos of sweet treats, which would then whoosh straight out of the door to houses across the community. These were long days of cooking but they bring back very happy memories. It was when the deli was fully stocked up with delights ready to show off to everyone that I would feel most proud. We gave out little tasters and I loved hearing the 'oooohs' and 'aaahhs' at the detail and intricacy of the dishes on offer. When you get that kind of reaction to your food, you just know that you've created something really special.

These types of celebratory snacks have never been on the restaurant menu at Prashad. And while the history behind these dishes will evoke certain emotions for Indians, these snacks will still taste spectacular. Not everything in this chapter has to be part of a big celebration or feast, though; I hope it inspires you to try something new and exciting, even when it isn't a special occasion. Or why not make up a reason and just celebrate it being the end of the week or the start of a new venture?

This kind of food isn't just something you knock together; the cooking should be as much of an experience as the eating. So save these dishes for when you have time to step back from the bustle of everyday life to really enjoy the creative process. I hope you have fun exploring this chapter, and use it to create some truly happy memories.

CHAKRI STRIPS ⟨ crispy rice and potato snacks

(V, WF, OG, N)

These intricate snacks are traditionally made into perfect swirls, but I like to focus on the taste and texture and not worry too much about the shape, so mine usually turn out more like crispy chips. They're served with tea and brunch during Diwali and other celebrations. This delicious recipe makes a large batch, which you can keep for guests to snack on.

MAKES A LARGE BATCH (ABOUT 1KG)

300g rice flour, sieved
1 medium red-skinned (or other waxy) potato, peeled, boiled and grated
6 cloves, toasted in a dry frying pan and crushed into a fine powder using a pestle and mortar
2½ tsp salt
½ tsp turmeric
25g sesame seeds
2 tsp medium red chilli powder
25ml sunflower oil, plus more for deep-frying
200ml warm water

First, if you don't have a steamer, you can create a makeshift one by balancing a plate on top of a flat-based heatproof bowl in a large pan of boiling water, three-quarters covered with a lid. The water should be 1–2cm below the lip of the bowl. Be careful not to let the lid slip fully onto the pan, as the water will boil over.

Pour the rice flour onto a muslin cloth and tie into a bundle. Place in the steamer (or on the plate). Steam on a medium heat for 15 minutes.

Tip the rice flour out of the muslin cloth into a large bowl. Break it up if it is lumpy. Add the grated potato, ground cloves, salt, turmeric, sesame seeds and chilli powder and mix well. Mix in the 25ml of sunflower oil and the warm water. Transfer to a piping bag with a 7mm star-shaped metal nozzle.

Heat the frying oil – about 10cm deep – in a large pan over a high heat (or in a deep fat fryer) and when you think it is hot enough, test the temperature by dropping a little of the dough into the oil; the pieces should quickly spring back up to float on the surface. Reduce the heat to medium. Pipe strips of random length into the oil and fry for 2 minutes. Remove the strips with a slotted spoon and lay them on absorbent kitchen towel. You will end up with crispy, delicately spiced, chip-shaped snacks. Anyone who is lucky enough to be around while these are being made can have a warm chewy one, before the *chakri* cools and hardens.

Store in an airtight container. Serve with *masala chai* (page 247) and some festive bites – such as *kakra bhajia* (page 221) and *bataka chevda* (page 174).

BATAKA CHEVDA 〈 Kaushy's Bombay mix

(V, WF, OG)

Bataka chevda is my version of Bombay mix. In the early days of the deli, I only made this special snack at home, but once people started to get a taste of it, we often ended up in celebration season fulfilling orders of up to 150 kilos! Rather than buying the ready-made mixture, have a go at making your own to serve in small bowls at your next family party. Trust me, your guests will taste the difference. This will keep for weeks in an airtight container – perfect for those unexpected visitors – but it is likely to get eaten up much sooner than that.

**MAKES A LARGE BATCH
(ABOUT 3KG)**

5 large red-skinned (or other waxy) potatoes, peeled and coarsely grated in long strips
sunflower oil for deep-frying, plus 75ml
150g red-skinned peanuts
105g cashew nuts
50g almonds
50g sultanas
8 fresh green chillies (ideally Kenyan), cut in ½cm dice
30g thick flattened rice (*pauwa*)
2 tsp turmeric
2 tsp medium red chilli powder
2 tsp salt
4 tsp sugar
15g white poppy seeds
2 tsp mustard seeds
½ tsp asafetida
25 fresh curry leaves, washed

Wash the potato strips in a sieve and drain. Take handfuls of the potato and squeeze out as much water as possible, then leave to dry on absorbent kitchen towel.

Now make sure you have a very large mixing bowl to hand, to put the various elements into as they are cooked. Heat the frying oil – about 10cm deep – in a large pan over a high heat (or in a deep fat fryer, if you have one) and when you think it is hot enough, test the temperature by dropping a little of the potato into the oil. When it is up to temperature, the potato will quickly spring back up to float on the surface. Reduce the heat to medium.

Fry the shredded potatoes in batches for 11 minutes until golden and crisp, stirring with a wooden or heatproof plastic spoon throughout. Remove from the oil with a slotted spoon and place on absorbent kitchen towel to drain. Bring the oil back up to temperature in between batches. Repeat until all the potato strips are fried. Tip the fried strips into the large mixing bowl.

Turn the frying oil to low and add the peanuts. Fry for 5 minutes, until some start rising to the top. Remove from the oil with a slotted spoon and put in the bowl with the potatoes. Repeat with the cashew nuts (fry for 2 minutes) and then with the almonds (fry for 2½ minutes). Add them to the mixing bowl too.

Using a deep metal sieve, dip the sultanas into the hot, bubbling oil for 40 seconds then tip them into the mixing bowl. Repeat the process with the chopped chillies. Put one handful of the flattened rice into the sieve and dip into the oil for a few seconds. It will immediately froth and increase in size. Tip the puffed rice into the mixing bowl and fry the rest of the rice, one handful at a time. Be careful with this dip-frying process, as the sultanas, chillies and rice will burn quickly.

Add the turmeric, chilli powder, salt, sugar and poppy seeds to the bowl. Use a large mixing spoon (I like to use a slotted one) to combine everything gently, folding the flavours through but taking care not to break the potato strips.

Heat the 75ml of oil in a small pan on a medium heat for 1 minute. Add the mustard seeds and when they start to pop, swirl in the asafetida. At arm's length, add the curry leaves and stir through. Empty the contents of the pan into the mixing bowl. Stir thoroughly and leave to cool. The flavours will develop as it cools.

Store in an airtight container and serve in small bowls. It will keep for 2–3 weeks… if you can make it last that long.

CHORA FARI ⟨ spicy 'poppadom' crisps

(V, WF, OG, N)

These crispy, savoury snacks look very much like poppadoms. Huge amounts of effort go into making them but they are devoured within seconds. The dough needs to be beaten really well to make it as light as possible, so that when you fry these they are full of air. My daughter-in-law, Minal, says that when you're exhausted and think you have beaten it as much as you possibly can, you are only halfway there. When Mohan and I ran our deli, we had a customer who would ask us to call her when these were being made, as she would buy 60–70 at a time for her husband to eat like crisps.

MAKES 20-25

120ml water
½ tsp bicarbonate of soda
1 tsp salt
260g gram (chickpea) flour, sieved
65g white lentil flour, sieved
2 tsp sunflower oil, plus more
   for frying
2 tsp medium red chilli powder
1 tsp Indian black salt

Put the water in a thick-based pan and bring to the boil on a medium heat. Dissolve the bicarbonate of soda and salt in the water. Transfer to another pan and sit it in some cold water to cool this as quickly as possible.

Pour the flours onto a tray and make a well in the middle. Pour the cooled soda-salt water and 2 teaspoons of oil into the well and mix together into a stiff dough.

You now need to beat and fold the dough to get plenty of air into it. Place the tray on the floor and hit the dough with a lightly-oiled heavy pestle (or a large oiled rolling pin) until it is flat – I find that 4 or 5 good thumps are enough to flatten it. Fold and shape the dough into a ball, replace on the tray and then beat flat again. Repeat this thumping, flattening, folding and shaping process at least 10 times, and keep going until the dough is light and airy.

Place the dough on a clear work surface, smooth a little oil over it, then roll it into a 2½cm-diameter sausage shape. Cut into 2cm pieces. Roll each piece into very thin 15cm-diameter discs on greaseproof paper. Make three parallel 8cm incisions on each piece of rolled-out dough, staying 3cm from the edge.

Heat the frying oil – about 10cm deep – in a large pan over a high heat (or in a deep fat fryer, if you have one) and when you think it is hot enough, test the temperature by dropping a little of the dough

CONTINUED OVERLEAF

into the oil. When it is up to temperature, the pieces will quickly spring back up to float on the surface. Reduce the heat to medium.

Drop the dough discs into the oil one at a time and fry for no more than 25 seconds – air pockets will pop up straight away. Take out of the oil using a slotted spoon or spatula and place on absorbent kitchen towel. Mix the chilli powder and black salt together and sprinkle onto the freshly fried *chora fari*. Repeat until they are all fried and seasoned.

Once cooled, place in an airtight container. Serve to guests to snack on when they visit, or just keep to eat as a snack whenever you fancy. These will keep for 2–3 weeks but are likely to be munched up well before that.

KAKADHIA ⟨ crisp sugar biscuits

(OG)

This is an iconic Diwali snack that you will only see around the festival. They are sweet and delicious. If your family is anything like mine, you'll find that everyone will loiter around while these are being made and keep nibbling until they are all gone.

MAKES 35

175ml milk
50ml cold water
30g sesame seeds
80g sugar
130g plain flour, sieved
55g *ghee* (or clarified butter), melted
sunflower oil for frying

Heat the milk, water and sesame seeds in a large thick-based pan on a medium heat for 5 minutes. Take off the heat and leave to cool until you can comfortably put your finger into it, then add the sugar and stir until dissolved. Pour the mixture into a measuring jug. There should be about 250ml.

Tip the flour into a large, shallow flat-based bowl or onto a baking tray and make a well in the middle. Pour the melted *ghee* into the well and mix in. Give the milk mixture a good stir, then pour 170ml of it into the tray (you can discard the rest). Knead into a stiff dough. Divide into 35 balls and use a rolling pin to roll each ball into a 10cm-diameter disc on greaseproof paper. Leave to dry for 1½ hours, making sure they are not overlapping. Turn them over, then leave for a further 45 minutes so that all the moisture dries off.

Heat the frying oil – about 10cm deep – in a large pan over a high heat (or in a deep fat fryer, if you have one) and when you think it is hot enough, test the temperature by dropping a little of the dough into the oil. When it is up to temperature, the pieces will quickly spring back up to float on the surface. Reduce the heat to medium.

Drop 4 discs into the oil and fry for 30 seconds on each side, turning with a wooden or heatproof plastic spoon and keeping the pieces separate from each other. Take out of the oil using a slotted spoon or spatula and place on absorbent kitchen towel. Repeat until you've fried all the dough.

Try a couple while they're warm (this isn't strictly necessary, but is very nice), then leave them to cool. Transfer to an airtight container and try to save some for guests. Good luck with that…

BHAKAR VADI ⟨ sweet and tangy fried rolls

(v, og)

These are a bit like spicy mini Swiss rolls, made from pastry and stuffed with a sweet, nutty filling that has a zing of chilli and ginger. They're a unique Diwali snack and I don't know of anything similar in other cultures and cuisines. My husband Mohan perfected this recipe when we ran our deli – but I took all the credit from the customers!

MAKES 22

Masala
8–10 fresh green chillies (ideally Kenyan)
4cm root ginger, peeled
pinch of salt

Filling
100g grated fresh coconut (or 80g unsweetened desiccated coconut)
50g red-skinned peanuts, coarsely blended
15g white poppy seeds
1 handful fresh coriander, washed and finely chopped
2 tsp salt
2½ tsp *garam masala*
juice of 1 lime
50g sesame seeds, toasted in a dry frying pan and cooled
60g sugar
2 tsp fennel seeds

Dough
260g gram (chickpea) flour, sieved
75g plain flour, sieved, plus extra to dust worktop and seal the rolls
1½ tsp salt
1 tsp medium red chilli powder
1 tsp turmeric
½ tsp asafetida

Crush the chillies and ginger together with a pinch of salt using a pestle and mortar (or a blender), to make a fine masala paste. Mix the masala paste with the filling ingredients in a large bowl and set aside to infuse.

Mix the gram flour, plain flour, salt, chilli powder, turmeric, asafetida and oil in a large bowl. Make a well in the middle, pour in the warm water and knead into a firm dough. Leave to rest for 5 minutes, then split into two pieces (about 208g each). Dust your worktop with flour and use a rolling pin to roll each dough piece until it is 3mm thick and roughly 28cm x 28cm. Smooth half a teaspoon of oil over each dough square.

Spread half the filling over one square, covering right up to the edges. Gently lift the edge closest to you and fold it over, then delicately roll into a spiral, ensuring that you don't squash the filling out of the sides. Repeat with the other square.

Use a sharp knife to cut each dough roll into 11 slices (each about 1½cm thick) so that you end up with 22 slices in total. Dab the cut ends with some plain flour to seal in the filling.

Heat the frying oil – about 10cm deep – in a large pan over a high heat (or in a deep fat fryer, if you have one) and when you think it is hot enough, test the temperature by dropping a little of the dough into the oil. When it is up to temperature,

30ml sunflower oil, plus 1 tsp to oil the dough, and more for frying

90ml warm water

the pieces will quickly spring back up to float on the surface. Reduce the heat to medium.

Drop 4–5 slices into the oil and fry for 3½ minutes. Take out of the oil using a slotted spoon or spatula and place on absorbent kitchen towel. Repeat until all the slices are fried.

Leave to cool, then store in an airtight container to serve to festive guests or family members when they fancy a sweet treat.

UNDHIYU ⟨ classic Gujarati mixed vegetable pot (V, WF, N)

If there were any dish you would expect from a Gujarati chef, it would be this. The complex ingredients and flavours combine to create something really special, and probably like nothing you've ever experienced before. When I lived in India, to mark the end of the rainy season we'd fast for seven days. At the end we'd feast all night on dishes like this one, as well as pastries, sweets and fruit salads. I remember sitting with all my best friends watching our favourite Bollywood films late into the night while eating this aromatic dish.

SERVES 4

Masala
4–6 fresh green chillies (ideally Kenyan)
4–6 cloves of garlic, soaked and peeled
5cm root ginger, peeled
pinch of salt

200ml sunflower oil
1 tsp mustard seeds
4 tsp carom seeds
1 tsp asafetida
300g frozen *papdi lilva* (Indian broad beans), thawed
2½ tsp salt
1¾ tsp turmeric
400ml boiling water
280g baby new potatoes
600g sweet potatoes, washed (but not peeled), topped, tailed and cut in 6cm x 3cm dice
20g sesame seeds
20g desiccated coconut
4 tsp sugar
2 handfuls of fresh coriander, washed and finely chopped
1 large aubergine (about 200g)
1 x 14cm purple yam, peeled, topped, tailed and cut in 6cm x 3cm dice (about 220g)
1 large banana, skin on, cut in 4cm slices
lemon wedges, to serve

Crush the chillies, garlic and ginger together with a pinch of salt using a pestle and mortar (or a blender), to make a fine masala paste.

Heat the oil in a deep (approx. 22cm) thick-based pan on a medium heat for 2 minutes. Add the mustard seeds and when they start to pop, swirl the carom seeds through for 30 seconds. Stir in the asafetida and allow the flavours to infuse for 30 seconds, then stir in the *papdi lilva* and cook for 1½ minutes. Add the salt and turmeric, stir, cover and allow to cook for 2½ minutes. Pour in 300ml of boiling water, re-cover and cook for 1 minute, then turn the heat down slightly and leave to simmer for 4 minutes.

Stir in the new potatoes and sweet potatoes, followed by the masala paste, sesame seeds and coconut. Add the sugar, stir, cover and cook for 5 minutes. Then stir in a handful of the fresh coriander, re-cover and cook for 3 minutes.

Now chop the aubergines into 4cm cubes. Add to the pan along with the purple yam, stir, cover and leave to cook for 16 minutes, stirring through gently every 3–4 minutes. Reduce the heat to low, stir in the final 100ml of boiling water and the banana, re-cover and cook for 7 minutes. Take off the heat and garnish with the remaining coriander. Leave to rest covered for 15 minutes.

Re-heat and serve piping hot with lemon wedges.

NOTE: *Don't cut the aubergine until it is time to add it and leave the banana skin on while it cooks so that the banana doesn't disintegrate (but do remember to remove the skin before eating).*

VEGETABLE KOFTA ⟨ vegetable patties in coriander, garlic and tomato sauce (v)

I can remember the day well: we were at Gordon Ramsay's Royal Hospital Road restaurant in London, competing for the Ramsay's Best Restaurant title in 2010. The pressure was huge. Minal and I really wanted to impress Gordon with a complexity of flavours and textures, so we chose this vegetable kofta, and it went down a treat. This is the perfect dish for a special occasion to wow even the pickiest of guests.

SERVES 4

Masala for filling – crush together using a pestle and mortar (or a blender), to make a fine paste

1–2 fresh green chillies (ideally Kenyan)
1–2 cloves of garlic, soaked and peeled
1½cm root ginger, peeled
pinch of salt

Filling

50g frozen peas, thawed and coarsely blended
½ medium carrot, peeled and coarsely blended
60g cauliflower florets, coarsely blended
70g white cabbage, coarsely blended
6 cashew nuts, coarsely blended
½ tsp lemon juice
1½ tsp salt
¼ tsp turmeric
1 handful fresh coriander, washed and finely chopped

Casing

3 medium red-skinned (or other waxy) potatoes, boiled, peeled and mashed
4 tsp plain flour, sieved
4 tsp gram (chickpea) flour, sieved
3 tsp cornflour, sieved

Put all the filling ingredients, including the filling masala paste, in a large bowl and gently but thoroughly mix everything together. The filling is all about texture, so don't overwork it. Lightly oil your hands and make 16 balls of about 2cm in diameter. Compress these quite tightly without crushing the vegetables and set aside in a tray.

Mix the mashed potato, flours, cornflour and salt together in a bowl with your hands (I wear catering gloves coated with oil, but you can just oil your hands if you prefer). Make sure the flours are well mixed into the potato. Keeping your hands/gloves well oiled, divide the potato mixture into 16 chunks of approximately 30g each. Roll each chunk gently in your hands and then flatten and pat down so each one fills the palm of your hand and is approximately ½cm thick.

Take a *kofta* filling ball and place in the middle of a potato patty. Gently fold over the edges of the potato mix to cover the *kofta* ball. Nip all the cracks together so that there are no gaps in the potato casing, and work the ball into shape using the palms of your hands. Repeat until all the *kofta* balls are finished.

Heat the frying oil – about 10cm deep – in a large pan over a high heat (or in a deep fat fryer, if you have one) and when you think it is hot enough, test the temperature by dropping a little of the *kofta* mixture into the oil. When it is up to temperature, the pieces will quickly spring back up to float on the surface. Reduce the heat to medium.

1 tsp salt

about 50ml sunflower oil to coat your hands/gloves, plus more for deep-frying

Masala for sauce – crush together using a pestle and mortar (or a blender), to make a fine paste

2–4 fresh green chillies (ideally Kenyan)

3–4 cloves of garlic, soaked and peeled

2cm root ginger, peeled

pinch of salt

Sauce

125ml sunflower oil

2 tsp cumin seeds

1 large onion, peeled and blended to a paste

240g peeled plum tomatoes, blended to pulp

2¼ tsp salt

2½ tsp turmeric

1½ tsp medium red chilli powder

3½ tsp ground coriander

½ tsp ground cumin

1 handful fresh coriander, washed and finely chopped

pinch of sugar

600ml boiling water

1 tsp *garam masala*

Gently place about 5 *koftas* at a time in the oil and stir using a wooden or heatproof plastic spoon until they are golden brown (roughly 3–5 minutes). Remove from the oil with a slotted spoon or strainer and leave to rest on absorbent kitchen towel while you fry the next batch. Repeat until all the *koftas* have been fried, then leave to cool.

Heat the oil in a thick-based pan on a medium heat, then swirl in the cumin seeds and let them gently froth. Just as they start to go brown, carefully add the onion paste, stir and cook for 10 minutes until it goes dark brown. Turn the heat to low and carefully add the blended tomatoes. Gently stir and simmer for 1 minute. Add the salt, turmeric, chilli powder, ground coriander, ground cumin, fresh coriander, sugar and the sauce masala paste. Mix through and cook for 1 minute, bringing all the spices and flavours together.

Now loosen the sauce with the boiling water. Three-quarters cover the pan and cook on a medium heat for 7 minutes. Stir in the *garam masala* and cook for 1 minute before gently adding the *koftas*. Make sure all the *koftas* are covered with sauce, then remove from the heat. Cover the pan and leave to rest for 15 minutes.

Reheat for 10 minutes on a very low heat before serving carefully, making sure the *koftas* don't break. If you're planning on cooking this dish in advance, don't add the *koftas* to the sauce until 10–15 minutes before you are ready to serve so they don't disintegrate.

Serve with *palak puri* (page 219), *jeera baath* (page 214) and finely chopped red salad onions.

DHAL BHATI & CHURMA *lentil soup with sweet and savoury dumplings*

Ramesh, who works alongside Minal in the kitchen at Prashad, has introduced us to lots of traditional Rajasthani cooking, including this special dish. As a taste experience, it's got a bit of everything. The dumplings are a lovely combination of sweet and savoury, and are rich from the buttery ghee. *I believe that when we cook, we mix a bit of love into the food as well, so using your hands to cook – as here, when you knead the dough and roll the dumplings – means the love is transferred more directly. And we all know that food made with love tastes so much better. This certainly isn't a low-fat dish… but it does taste wonderful.*

SERVES 4

Bhati
350g chapatti flour, sieved
1 tsp salt
60g *ghee* (or clarified butter),
  melted, plus 25g to brush on top
  of the dough balls
120ml warm water

Churma
175g chapatti flour, sieved
50g *ghee* (or clarified butter),
  melted, plus 25g to brush on top
  of the dough balls
90ml water
30g almonds, finely blended
30g cashew nuts, finely blended
130g *jaggery*, finely sliced (or
  demerara / soft brown sugar)
1 tsp ground cardamom
about 50g white poppy seeds,
  for dipping

Masala
4–6 fresh green chillies (ideally
  Kenyan)
3cm root ginger, peeled
pinch of salt

Mix the chapatti flour and salt for the *bhati* in a large bowl. Add the melted *ghee* and mix through. Pour in the water, mix with your hands and knead into a firm dough. Break into 12 equal pieces of approximately 45g each. Roll each into a ball, then slightly press to flatten and place on a baking tray. Brush the *bhati* with the additional melted *ghee*.

Mix the chapatti flour for the *churma* with 50g melted *ghee* and the water in a large bowl and knead until you have a firm dough. Split into 8 pieces of approximately 35g each and roll into balls. Lay on the baking tray with the *bhati*, making sure you can distinguish one from the other. Brush the tops of the *churma* with the additional melted *ghee*.

Bake the *bhati* and *churma* balls for 30 minutes in a preheated oven at 250°C/230°C fan/gas mark 9 (or hotter if your oven has a higher setting – I use 250°C fan). Take out and leave to cool for 10 minutes.

Place the 8 *churma* balls in a blender and blitz to a fine breadcrumb-like mixture. Tip into a large bowl and mix in the almonds and cashew nuts. Heat the *jaggery* in a small non-stick frying pan on a medium heat for 1½ minutes until melted. Pour the melted *jaggery* into the crumbed *churma*-nut mixture and mix everything together with a wooden or heatproof plastic spoon. Once it's cool enough to handle, add the ground cardamom and mix through with your hands.

Dhal

250g *mung dhal* (yellow split
mung beans), soaked in 1 ltr
hot water for 40 minutes

800ml boiling water

4 tsp sunflower oil, plus 50ml
for frying

1 tsp mustard seeds

½ tsp asafetida

5 cloves of garlic, soaked, peeled
and finely chopped

2 medium vine tomatoes, cut in
1cm dice

1½ tsp turmeric

2 tsp ground coriander

½ tsp ground cumin

3 tsp salt

1 handful fresh coriander, washed
and finely chopped

Now wet your hands with a little water and compress the mixture into 8 dough balls of approximately 55g each. It will be quite difficult because of the flaky texture, but the heat from your hands will soften up the *jaggery*, making the mixture sticky. Dip the top of each dough ball into the poppy seeds (I put them in a small bowl) and set aside.

Drain the soaked *dhal* and put in a thick-based pan. Add 500ml of boiling water and 4 teaspoons of sunflower oil and bring to a simmer on full heat. Reduce the heat to low and cook uncovered for 10 minutes, stirring occasionally. Add another 200ml of boiling water and simmer for a further 10 minutes. Take off the heat and set aside (do not drain).

Crush the chillies, garlic and ginger together with a pinch of salt using a pestle and mortar (or a blender), to make a fine masala paste.

Heat the 50ml sunflower oil in a thick-based frying pan on a high heat for 1½ minutes. Add the mustard seeds and when they start to pop, swirl in the asafetida and garlic and cook for 30 seconds. Add the masala paste and stir through the oil for 10 seconds, then turn the heat down to low and fry for 30 seconds. Add the tomatoes, stir through and cook on a high heat for 2 minutes. Stir in the turmeric, ground coriander, ground cumin and salt. Cook for 1 minute before reducing the heat back to low and leaving to cook for 4 minutes. Stir the remaining 100ml of boiling water into the *dhal*, then tip the *dhal* and its liquid into the frying pan. Add the fresh coriander and stir through. Cook for 2 minutes on a low heat. Take off the heat, cover and leave to rest for 10 minutes.

Serve the *dhal* in large bowls, with the savoury *bhati* and sweet *churma* dough balls on the side to dip in.

DUM BIRYANI *⌇ layered vegetable rice*

(WF, N, HO)

The 'dum' in the title of this recipe refers to the process of sealing the pot that the biryani is cooked in, in order to trap all the flavours into the rice. To do this, I make a seal all around the edge of the pot with some dough, and I don't break it until I serve the biryani at the table so that all the wonderful aromas come spilling out. In India, Minal learnt to cook this in a big pot over an open fire in the garden. It is the dish she cooked at the regional finals of ITV's 2011 Britain's Best Dish, *and the judges loved it so much they couldn't stop eating it!*

SERVES 4

300g rice (ideally Tilda basmati),
  soaked in water for 30 minutes
1 tsp salt
2 tsp sunflower oil
100g red-skinned (or other waxy)
  potatoes, peeled and cut in 1cm
  dice

Masala
2–4 fresh green chillies (ideally
  Kenyan)
4–5 cloves of garlic, soaked and
  peeled
5cm root ginger, peeled
pinch of salt

Vegetable mixture
55ml sunflower oil, plus 25ml
3cm cinnamon stick
2 Indian bay leaves, washed
4 peppercorns
seeds of 1 cardamom pod
2 cloves
1 tsp cumin seeds
½ tsp asafetida
12 fresh curry leaves, washed
1 medium onion, cut in 1cm dice
2 carrots, peeled and cut in
  1½cm dice

Drain the rice and put in a thick-based pan. Cover with boiling water, then add the salt, oil and potatoes and cook uncovered on a medium heat for 4½ minutes. Reduce the heat to low, cover and cook for 1 minute. Take off the heat and leave to rest uncovered.

Crush the chillies, garlic and ginger together with a pinch of salt using a pestle and mortar (or a blender), to make a fine masala paste.

Heat 55ml of the sunflower oil in a large thick-based frying pan on a high heat for 1½ minutes, then add the cinnamon and swirl through the oil for 30 seconds. Add the bay leaves, peppercorns, cardamom seeds and cloves and swirl through the oil for a further 30 seconds. Stir in the cumin seeds and asafetida, then, at arm's length, add the curry leaves – watch out for spitting from the moisture. Add the onion, keep stirring, and fry for 30 seconds until it is sizzling. Stirring continuously, add the carrots (fry for 1 minute), then the French beans and asparagus (fry for 1 minute), then the broccoli and cauliflower (1½ minutes), the aubergine and courgette (1 minute) and the pepper (1 minute). Finally, stir in the peas, masala paste, salt, turmeric and *garam masala* and cook for 1 minute. Remove from the heat, stir in the lime juice and fresh coriander and leave to rest uncovered.

Put the remaining 25ml of sunflower oil in a large deep thick-based pan. Put a generous portion

50g French beans, topped, tailed
 and cut in 1cm dice
6 asparagus spears, trimmed
 and cut in 1cm dice
50g broccoli, cut in 1cm dice
70g cauliflower, cut in 1cm dice
1 aubergine, cut in ½cm dice
½ courgette, cut in 1½cm dice
½ red pepper, cut in 1cm dice
50g frozen peas, thawed
2 tsp salt
1 tsp turmeric
1 tsp *garam masala*
juice of ½ lime
1 handful fresh coriander,
 washed and finely chopped

Dough to seal
100g chapatti flour, sieved
60ml warm water

(roughly a third) of the vegetable mixture in a layer at the bottom and follow with a layer of rice (again about a third). Repeat twice so that you have 3 layers of vegetables and 3 layers of rice. Cover and leave to rest while you make the dough.

Put the chapatti flour in a large mixing bowl and create a well in the middle. Pour the water into the well and mix together with your hands. Knead the dough. Squeeze into a long thin sausage shape with your hands and use it to seal the join between the edge of the large pan and the lid. Make sure it is fully airtight all the way round, then set on a low heat to cook for 15 minutes. Don't break the seal or uncover the pan. Leave to rest for 10 minutes.

Bring the pan to the table, break the seal and serve hearty portions accompanied by *chana chaat patti* (page 244).

HYDERABADI BIRYANI & vegetable rice with mint masala

(WF, OG, N)

Ghee isn't an ingredient that we use often, as it is rather rich for everyday meals but this particular biryani is known throughout the whole of India. It is special because of the unique flavours that come from the famous Hyderabadi masala, which combines fresh mint with dried red chillies, poppy seeds and coconut. It's a dish your guests won't forget.

SERVES 4

250g rice (ideally Tilda basmati),
  soaked in cold water for half an hour

Hyderabadi masala
20g butter
2 dried red chillies, split in half
3 tsp white poppy seeds
½ tsp turmeric
30g desiccated coconut
8 fresh mint leaves, washed and
  finely chopped

2 carrots, peeled
85g broccoli
55g French beans
6 asparagus spears, trimmed
½ red pepper
½ aubergine (approx. 60g)
½ courgette
30g *ghee* (or clarified butter)
4cm cinnamon stick
2 Indian bay leaves, washed
5 black peppercorns
seeds from 2 cardamom pods
2 tsp *garam masala*
2 tsp salt
1 tsp medium red chilli powder
½ tsp dried fenugreek leaves
½ tsp turmeric
1 handful fresh coriander, washed
  and finely chopped

Drain the rice and put in a large thick-based pan with 460ml of boiling water. Cover and cook on a high heat for 15 minutes. Take off the heat and leave to cool.

Melt the butter for the *Hyderabadi masala* in a thick-based frying pan on a low heat for 40 seconds. Swirl the dried red chillies through the melted butter, then add the poppy seeds. Add the turmeric, coconut, mint and ½ teaspoon of salt and stir for 1½ minutes. Take off the heat and leave to cool.

Cut all the vegetables into 1cm dice. Melt the *ghee* in a thick-based frying pan on a medium heat for 1 minute and swirl it around the base of the pan. Stir the cinnamon into the *ghee*. Turn the heat up to high, then mix in the bay leaves, peppercorns and cardamom seeds and fry for 30 seconds. Stir in the carrots and fry for 30 seconds, then the broccoli (45 seconds), French beans (30 seconds), asparagus (30 seconds) and pepper (30 seconds). Add the aubergine and courgette, reduce the heat to medium, stir and fry for 3½ minutes, before covering and leaving to cook for 1 minute.

Give the vegetables a good stir, add the *garam masala*, salt, chilli powder, fenugreek leaves and turmeric, then stir again. Sprinkle the fresh coriander on top and remove the pan from the heat. Empty the rice into the vegetable pan and gently stir through. Finally stir in the *Hyderabadi masala*, then cover and leave to rest for 10 minutes.

Serve with *bhinda* fries (page 223) and *mitu gajar murabho* (page 233).

GOOGRA ⟨ spiced nut parcels

These intricate little parcels are rich and sugary. They traditionally have an amazing decorative seal, like a rope running around the edge, but for practical reasons I have recommended an easier crimp-seal here. When cooking, they give off a delicious aroma so I turn off the extractor fan and let the smell fill the house. My family are only allowed them during Diwali and I suggest you save them for special occasions too.

MAKES 20

Filling
130g *ghee* (or clarified butter)
250g fine semolina
80g gram (chickpea) flour, sieved
40g almonds, finely ground
10g pistachios, finely ground
4g grated nutmeg
1½ tsp ground cardamom
200g sugar

Casing
400g plain flour, sieved
12g fine semolina
60g *ghee* (or clarified butter),
  melted, plus extra to coat
140ml milk
50ml cold water
sunflower oil for frying

Melt 60g of the *ghee* for the filling in a thick-based pan on a medium heat. Add the semolina and toast for 11 minutes until light brown in colour, stirring every 20 seconds to ensure that it doesn't burn. Take off the heat and leave to cool (near an open window or porch, if you have one). Go back to it and stir every so often.

Melt the other 70g of *ghee* in a small thick-based pan on a medium heat. Add the gram flour and toast on a low heat for 1 minute, stirring regularly and breaking it up with a spatula to make sure it toasts evenly. Gently cook for 5 minutes, until you have a runny mixture. Take off the heat and gently stir in the semolina, almonds, pistachios, nutmeg and cardamom. Leave to cool until you can put your finger in – it should be cool but not cold. Mix the sugar in with your hands until it is fully incorporated – it should still be grainy, rather than sticky or melted. Set aside.

Put the flour and semolina for the casing in a large bowl and create a well in the middle. Pour the melted *ghee* into the well and mix through. Warm the milk and cold water together in a pan to roughly blood temperature. Pour into the flour mixture, then knead into a dough. Coat the dough with a little more melted *ghee* and split into 30 balls of roughly 20g each, then cover with a tea towel so they don't dry out.

Using a rolling pin, roll each piece into a 9½cm-diameter disc. Taking one disc at a time, spoon about 25g of the filling mixture into the middle, then fold into a half-moon-shape and nip the edges together. Make sure it is properly sealed by pressing the edges together with a fork, being careful not to pierce the dough. Repeat until all the discs are stuffed and sealed. Lay them in a tray and cover with a tea towel again (if they dry out, they may crack when frying).

Heat the frying oil – about 10cm deep – in a large pan over a high heat (or in a deep fat fryer, if you have one) and when you think it is hot enough, test the temperature by dropping a little of the dough into the oil. When it is up to temperature, the pieces will quickly spring back up to float on the surface. Reduce the heat to medium. Fry as many as you can fit in the pan at a time for 3 minutes. Take out of the oil with a slotted spoon and place on absorbent kitchen towel to cool.

Store in an airtight container and try to save some for guests.

INDIAN FRUIT SALAD (WF, N)

This sweet, refreshing pudding served cold straight from the fridge is the perfect end to a feast full of spices and intense flavours. Chikoo, also known as sapodilla, *are available from Indian stores, but if you can't track them down, you can use pears.*

SERVES 4

30g custard powder
1.5 ltr full fat milk
150g sugar
1 large apple, cut in ½cm dice
2 bananas, cut in ½cm dice
2 *chikoo*, seeds removed and flesh cut in ½cm dice
1 pear, cut in ½cm dice
1 handful grapes, quartered
seeds from ¼ pomegranate
2 tsp vanilla extract

Mix the custard powder with 100ml milk in a bowl or glass, making sure there are no lumps.

Heat the remaining milk in a thick-based pan on full heat, stirring every 30 seconds, until simmering (roughly 10 minutes). Add the custard paste and stir for 4 minutes, then tip in the sugar and cook for 6 minutes, stirring continuously. Take off the heat and put the pan in a bowl or sink of cold water for at least 3 minutes to cool. Keep stirring the mixture while it cools to avoid a skin developing on top.

Once the custard mixture is cold, stir in the fruit and vanilla extract, then refrigerate for at least 2 hours. Serve ice-cold, in deep bowls.

ANGUR RABRI ⟨ creamy milk pudding

(WF)

This is a traditional pudding popular throughout India. It is made up of two parts: one spongy and one milky. 'Angur' means grape and refers to the size and shape of the curd balls, which need to be absorbent to soak up the creamy cardamom rabri. In the days when we did a lot of catering, my husband, Mohan, was very proud of this dish because dairy was his domain. It is particularly close to his heart because he served it to 500 people at our daughter Hina's engagement party. It will keep for a day or two in an airtight container in the fridge if you want to make it in advance.

SERVES 5

Angur
1 ltr full fat milk
½ tsp citric acid
1 ltr water
100g sugar

Rabri
2 ltr full fat milk
125g sugar
½ tsp cardamom, coarsely ground

20 pistachios, coarsely ground,
  to serve

Heat the milk for the *angur* in a large thick-based pan on high for 7 minutes to bring it to the boil. Once it is boiling, stir in the citric acid and heat for 30 seconds before stirring again. Watch how the milk completely splits into curd and whey. Take off the heat again and drain away the whey, catching the curd in a sieve. Tip the curd into a pan of cold water for 2 minutes to cool.

Line a colander or sieve with muslin. Scoop the curd from the cold water and squeeze it a little before placing it on the muslin. Once all the curd is in the cloth, bundle it up and wring it out, twisting to get out as much of the water as possible. Tip the squeezed curd into a large bowl, then knead and stretch it until it is soft and spongy. Place on a board or clean work surface, roll into a 1½cm-diameter sausage, then cut into about 40 chunks (each about 1½cm x 1½cm).

Bring a litre of water to the boil in a large pan on high heat. Stir in the sugar, reduce the heat to medium and let the water simmer. Compress each chunk of spongy curd into a tight ball in your hand, then drop into the pan to absorb the sugar water. Leave to simmer in the pan for 14–15 minutes, then take out using a slotted spoon and drop into a bowl of cold water. Set aside (still in the water).

Heat the milk and sugar for the *rabri* in a large thick-based pan on a high heat for 11 minutes, stirring constantly to ensure that the milk doesn't stick. Reduce the heat to medium and simmer for 50 minutes to reduce the milk, stirring all the time to ensure that it doesn't catch on the bottom of the pan. Take off the heat and leave to cool.

Once the milk has cooled, stir in the cardamom and all the *angur* balls. Cover and chill in the fridge for at least a couple of hours, then serve with a generous sprinkling of pistachios on top. I like to serve this in Martini glasses so that you can see the texture of the pudding.

SEV ❦ sweet cardamom vermicelli
(N)

We Gujaratis have a sweet tooth and can't always wait for dessert. Sugary, creamy and delicious, this traditional pudding is actually served with the main meal and is a particular favourite of mine. In fact, if I had my way, I'd just sit and eat it on its own. You can enjoy it hot, cold or warm but I like it best when it is steaming hot. We used to eat this to celebrate the arrival of spring the day after having a big bonfire, but it's good at any time of year.

SERVES 4

200g *sev* (Indian vermicelli)
100g *ghee* (or clarified butter)
400ml milk
1¼ tsp ground cardamom
150g sugar

Break the *sev* into 3cm lengths. Fry the *sev* with the *ghee* in a thick-based frying pan over a medium heat for 1½ minutes. Turn the heat down, give it a stir and cook for another 5 minutes.

While the *sev* is cooking, gently bring the milk to the boil in a thick-based pan on a medium heat.

Carefully pour the milk onto the buttery *sev* in the frying pan. Stir together and cook on a low heat for 2 minutes. Stir in the cardamom and the sugar, mix everything together, and cook on a low heat for 6 minutes, stirring occasionally.

Take off the heat, stir once more and then serve, piping hot.

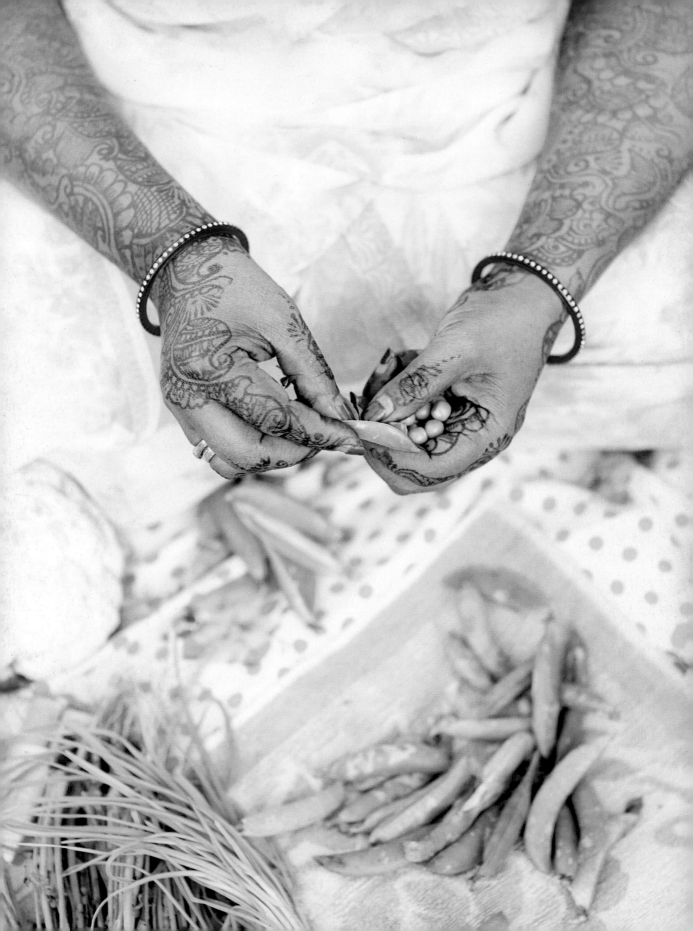

ALL THE EXTRAS

MAKAI ROTLA ⸏ healthy cornmeal flatbread

METHI BHAKRI ⸏ fenugreek flatbread

ROTLI ⸏ traditional puffed flatbread

BATHURA ⸏ fluffy fried fermented bread

TAMETA PILAU ⸏ fluffy tomato rice

TUVAR PILAU ⸏ pigeon pea rice

BAATH ⸏ boiled basmati rice

JEERA BAATH ⸏ cumin-infused rice

TUVAR DHAL KICHDI ⸏ pigeon peas and rice

PALAK PURI ⸏ spinach 'clouds'

KAKRA BHAJIA ⸏ paprika potato crisps

BHINDA FRIES ⸏ crispy okra chips

MASALA CHIPS

STICKY CHILLI CHIPS

KHUDI ⸏ spiced yoghurt soup

DHAL ⸏ traditional yellow lentil soup

SAMBAR ⸏ aromatic vegetable and lentil soup

MITU GAJAR MURABHO ⸏ sweet carrot pickle

KOPRU ⸏ mustard seed, curry leaf and coconut dip

SHIMLA MIRCH ⸏ red pepper and carrot relish

SAFARJAN WATTANA ⸏ apple and pea chutney

LASAN CHUTNEY ⸏ garlic and red chilli chutney

IMLI CHUTNEY ⸏ sweet and tangy tamarind chutney

BARELA MARCHA ⸏ chillies with sweet cumin satay

CHANA CHAAT PATTI ⸏ tangy chickpea salsa

MASALA CHAI ⸏ spicy tea

Indian meals are made of up lots of elements and you'll seldom find a table set without some kind of delicious accompaniment. We tend to serve breads and rice with the 'wet' dishes, to soak up all the lovely flavours; with dips, sauces and chutneys added to 'dry' dishes to give them a bit of moisture. They also serve to balance the flavours or temper the heat in certain dishes. For example, I might make a cooling, fresh relish to go with a particularly spicy curry, or a hot, fiery chilli dip to give a bit of a kick to a milder dish. It is traditional to eat Indian meals with your hands and we even have a saying: 'If you eat with a spoon, you feed your belly; if you eat with your hands, you feed your soul.' So there needs to be plenty of those all-important breads piled up, ready to scoop up every last bit of sauce. In this chapter you'll find all the extras you need for a fully authentic, well-rounded Gujarati feast.

Whilst they may be served 'on the side', a lot of effort goes into these accompaniments, and you can really taste it. There is a huge difference between ready-made chutneys from a jar and homemade ones using fresh ingredients. Although it may take a bit of extra time, it really is worth it, as it's so easy to ruin a carefully prepared meal with a cheap-tasting chutney or badly made bread. Once you've had the homemade version, I doubt you'll ever want to go back to the shop-bought one. The quality and freshness of your breads and rice is very important. I always try to time it just right so that they are hot and fluffy when they reach the table, ready for people to dig in.

Some of the recipes in this chapter are classics, which also appeared in my first cookbook. After all, there are some dishes, like fluffy *baath* rice (page 213), puffy *rotli* bread (page 206), traditional yellow lentil *dhal* (page 228) and a really great *imli* chutney (page 241), that I feel no Indian cookery book should be without, so they simply couldn't be left out of this one either. Some recipes, like *palak puri* (page 219), *tameta pilau* (page 211) and *makai rotla* (page 202), are variations on traditional accompaniments. And others, like the sticky chilli chips (page 225) and *bhinda* fries (page 223) are newer creations, designed specifically to go with the relaxed style of home-cooking that runs through this book.

Please don't feel that these breads, rice and side dishes are limited to being served with Indian cuisine, though. Many of them will complement flavours of foods from all around the world. As you saw in my Fusion chapter, I love combining ideas and ingredients and these can be a great way of adding a bit of Gujarati depth and spice to the table, without having to make a full meal. You'll find suggestions for what to serve them with throughout the book, but have some fun experimenting as well – I can testify that the *shimla mirch* (page 237), *lasan* chutney (page 239) and *imli* chutney (page 241) all go very well in a very British cheese sandwich!

MAKAI ROTLA ୬ healthy cornmeal flatbread

(V, WF, OG, N, HO)

Traditional rotla *was widely eaten when my mother's generation was growing up but it is less popular today. This is such a shame, as it is an excellent healthy bread made with just sorghum flour and water – there's nothing else to it. This spiced cornmeal version is a Punjabi village classic that you won't often see in UK restaurants. You can cook* rotla *in advance of the meal, then reheat before serving.*

MAKES 10

400g fine cornmeal, plus 50g for
  rolling
2 tsp salt
2 tsp medium red chilli powder
½ tsp turmeric
2 tsp cumin seeds
350ml boiling water

Mix the cornmeal, salt, chilli powder, turmeric and cumin seeds together in a large bowl. Add the water and mix the dough using a wooden or heatproof plastic spoon, working all the ingredients together. When the water has cooled enough, knead the dough with your hands and then divide it into 10 balls of approximately 90g each. Sprinkle a little flour onto your worktop to prevent sticking, then roll each dough ball into a 15cm-diameter disc. Don't worry too much about the shape, it is more important that the discs are of even thickness.

Heat your *tawa* or regular frying pan on a medium heat for 1 minute. Carefully place each *rotla* in the pan and dry fry for 1 minute, then turn over with a spatula and cook for a further 3½ minutes. Flip back over and cook for 1 minute, then turn over and press down with the spatula for 30 seconds. Finally, flip again and press down with the spatula for another minute before removing from the pan. You will need to work fast, because the *rotla* will start to go soft as soon as it comes out of the pan, so try using 2 frying pans at a time to get them all done quickly.

Serve warm on their own with butter, or as an accompaniment to dishes like *sukhu kobi wattana* (page 57) or *renghan bharta* (page 86).

METHI BHAKRI ᴄ fenugreek flatbread

(N)

Bobby loves these fenugreek-infused chapattis and if he is around when I'm making them, he'll just sit and eat them straight from the pan. They make a great savoury snack but they are also fantastic with any sauce. My granddaughter Maitri loves using my homemade breads to scoop up every last drop of her curry and always ends up with a smear of it (and a big smile) across her face.

MAKES 16

Masala
4–6 fresh green chillies (ideally Kenyan)
4–6 cloves of garlic, soaked and peeled
pinch of salt

75ml sunflower oil, plus 16 tsp for frying
2 tsp cumin seeds
8 tsp plain live set yoghurt
½ tsp turmeric
2 tsp salt
460g chapatti flour, sieved
125ml warm water
2 handfuls fresh fenugreek leaves, washed and coarsely chopped
2 tsp sugar

Crush the chillies and garlic together with a pinch of salt using a pestle and mortar (or a blender), to make a fine masala paste.

Mix the masala paste, 75ml of sunflower oil, cumin, yoghurt, turmeric, salt, flour, water, fenugreek leaves and sugar together in a large bowl. Knead the dough until it is firm, then divide it into 16 dough balls. Sprinkle a little flour onto your worktop to prevent sticking, then smooth the balls one at a time in the palm of your hands and flatten slightly before rolling into a 16cm-diameter disc. Don't worry too much about the shape, it is more important that the discs are of even thickness.

Heat your *tawa* or regular frying pan on a medium heat for 1 minute. Carefully place each *bhakri* in the pan and dry fry for 1 minute, then turn over with a spatula and cook for a further 3½ minutes. Flip back over and drizzle a teaspoon of oil around the edges of the pan, then cook for 1 minute and press down on the surface with the spatula for 30 seconds. Flip again and press down with the spatula for 1 minute, then take out of the pan. You will need to work fast, because the *bhakri* will start to go soft as soon as they come out of the pan, so try using 2 frying pans at a time to get them all done quickly.

Serve piping hot with *masala chai* (page 247) or *chana chaat patti* (page 244).

BATHURA

METHI BHAKRI

ROTLIS

MAKAI ROTLA

ROTLI ~ traditional puffed flatbread

(OG, N, HO)

Rotli are soft, thin, unleavened chapatti breads, traditionally used instead of a fork to pick up curry, dhal, pickles or anything else you happen to be eating. In Indian culture, we usually eat with our hands, so this is the perfect way to avoid too much mess – and you get to eat them at the same time! Rotli are cooked in two stages: first, they are sealed in a medium-hot pan or tawa and then they are puffed up directly over the heat source. I puff them up over a gas flame, but if you don't have a gas hob, you can cook the rotli on a round mesh screen with a handle (the type designed to stop fat or sauces spitting up while cooking) held over an electric hob, or you can put them in the microwave for 10–20 seconds on a low setting.

SERVES 4 (MAKES 16)

300g chapatti flour, sieved
50ml sunflower oil
300ml boiling water
butter for greasing

Put the flour in a large bowl, add the oil and boiling water, then stir with a spoon until the dough starts to come together and has cooled enough to start using your hands. Knead for at least 2–3 minutes. The more you work the dough, the softer and fluffier the *rotlis* will be. The dough will be quite sticky, so gently smooth the surface with lightly oiled hands, wrap in clingfilm and set aside until you are ready to cook the *rotlis*.

Divide in 16 roughly equal pieces (you can either judge by eye or, if you want to be more exact, weigh the dough and divide by 16 to calculate how much each piece should weigh). Form the dough pieces into balls between your palms and squash to flatten slightly. Put a flat *tawa* pan or a flat-based non-stick frying pan over a very low heat to warm while you roll the first *rotli* (*tawa* are traditionally very thick, so they take a while to heat up).

Dust a dough ball with chapatti flour (not too much or it will burn), place on a lightly floured work surface and use a rolling pin to flatten into a thin disc, about 19–20cm in diameter. Keep the pressure on the rolling pin light so that you can shape the *rotli* as you roll it, turning the dough 90° after every couple of rolls to keep it circular. Don't worry too much about the shape: it is more important that the disc is of even thickness – not thicker at the middle or edges – so that it will puff up properly. With practice you will acquire the knack of making perfectly round *rotli*. If you find the dough sticking to the worktop, lift it and sprinkle a little flour underneath before continuing to roll.

Increase the heat under the pan to medium, shake any excess flour off the *rotli* and place in the pan. After a minute or so it will start to bubble, cooking the outer layer and sealing it. Turn to seal the other side.

Remove the pan from the heat, increase the gas to high and use tongs to lay the *rotli* straight on the gas ring. As soon as it has puffed up, remove from the heat, place on absorbent kitchen towel and smear with a little butter to grease the surface and stop the next *rotli* from sticking to it. Repeat the sealing and puffing process until all the *rotlis* are cooked and stacked on top of each other. If you are making them in advance of serving, wrap in aluminium foil to stop them drying out. Serve while still warm or allow to cool (simply reheat in the pan for a minute or two over a medium heat before serving).

Rotlis can be served with pretty much any meal, but go particularly well with *karella na reveya* (page 80) or *dum aloo* (page 90). Any leftover *rotlis* can be stored in an airtight container (once they've cooled) and reheated in the *tawa* or frying pan the next day. Alternatively you can use them to make a variation on *vagarela tortillas* (page 128) for lunch or a light supper.

BATHURA ⟨ fluffy fried fermented bread

(OG, N)

Bathura is a Punjabi classic – delicious, soft, fluffy fried bread, made with a yoghurt-fermented dough. It is traditionally eaten with rich tomato and onion-based curries like rajma *(page 60) or* tameta reveya *(page 45). Try them together and you'll see why – the combination of the spice-infused tomato and the soft chewy bread is a match made in heaven. This bread is wonderful either warm or cold – if serving warm, fry at the last minute once everything else is ready.*

SERVES 4 (MAKES 16)

380g plain flour, sieved
20g *ghee* (or clarified butter), melted
50g plain live set yoghurt
1 tsp salt
1 tsp black peppercorns, coarsely ground or crushed
200ml soda water
sunflower oil for frying

Put the flour, *ghee*, yoghurt, salt and pepper in a large bowl and mix through. Add the soda water and stir until the dough starts to come together. Knead for at least 2 minutes, until firm. Put the dough in an airtight container and leave for at least an hour at room temperature while the fermenting yoghurt works its magic and causes the dough to rise slightly.

Divide the dough in 16 roughly equal pieces (you can either judge by eye or, if you want to be more exact, weigh the dough and divide by 16 to calculate how much each piece should weigh). Lightly oil your hands (this makes it easier to handle the sticky dough), then form the dough pieces into balls between your palms and squash to flatten slightly.

Place a flattened dough ball on a clean work surface and use a rolling pin to roll into a thin disc about 12cm in diameter. Keep the pressure on the rolling pin light so that you can shape the dough as you roll it. Turn the dough 90° after every couple of rolls to keep it circular. Don't worry too much about the shape: it is more important that the disc is of even thickness – not thicker at the middle or edges – so that it will puff up properly. In time you will acquire the knack of making it perfectly round. Repeat with the remaining dough balls, placing the discs on a lightly oiled baking sheet as you go, making sure not to overlap the edges to avoid them sticking together.

Heat the frying oil – about 10cm deep – in a large pan over a high heat (or in a deep fat fryer, if you have one) and when you think it is hot enough, test the temperature by sprinkling a few little pieces of dough in the oil. When it is up to temperature, the pieces will quickly spring back up to float on the surface.

Gently place a couple of *bathura* in the oil (I cook three or four at a time, but start with two if you haven't done this before). They will start to puff up within about 30 seconds. As soon as they do, use a heatproof spoon or ladle to turn them in the oil, then spoon oil over them to help them cook evenly. Fry for a further 15 seconds or so, until golden brown. Remove from the oil with a slotted spoon or strainer and leave to rest on absorbent kitchen towel while you fry the next batch. Repeat until all the *bathura* have been fried.

Serve warm or cold with *rajma* (page 60), *tameta reveya* (page 45) or any other rich tomato- and onion-based curry. Any left over can be stored in an airtight container once they've cooled, to be eaten cold the next day (I don't reheat them as I think it affects the flavour of the *ghee*).

TAMETA PILAU ⟨ fluffy tomato rice

(WF, N, HO)

This traditional rice dish is great for bringing moisture and texture to dry curries. Gujarati cooking is almost as much about appearance as taste, and the tomatoes here add a lovely pink colour that livens up the plate, providing a great contrast with the other elements of the meal. This is one of the most popular rice dishes in the Patel house and you'll see it suggested as an accompaniment for many of the dishes in this book.

SERVES 4

Masala
4–6 fresh green chillies (ideally Kenyan)
2–4 cloves of garlic, soaked and peeled
3cm root ginger, peeled
pinch of salt

50ml sunflower oil
1 tsp cumin seeds
300g basmati rice, gently washed and drained twice
1¼ tsp salt
3 medium vine tomatoes, blended to a fine pulp
45g butter
pinch of turmeric

Crush the chillies, garlic and ginger together with a pinch of salt using a pestle and mortar (or a blender), to make a fine masala paste.

Heat the oil in a thick-based pan for 1½ minutes. Add the cumin seeds and swirl through the oil for 30 seconds, then add the drained rice and enjoy the sizzle. Stir with a wooden or heatproof plastic spoon for 45 seconds, then add the masala paste and stir for 1 minute. Add the salt and stir for 1 minute before adding the tomatoes, butter and turmeric. Stir through gently and cook uncovered for 2 minutes.

Add 500ml of boiling water and stir for 45 seconds, until simmering. Cook with the lid half-covering the pan for 6–7 minutes, stirring every 2 minutes to ensure that the rice isn't sticking to the bottom of the pan, then reduce the heat to low and add 30ml of water. Put a large square of aluminium foil on top of the rice and tuck it into the edges of the pan to seal the rice in and keep it moist and fluffy while it steams. Cover with the lid, reduce the heat to the lowest setting and cook for 13–14 minutes. Take off the heat and leave to rest covered for 15 minutes.

Serve piping hot with *renghan lothiu* (page 34) or *karella na reveya* (page 80).

TUVAR PILAU ⟨ pigeon pea rice

(WF, N, HO)

Fresh or dried pigeon peas are very popular in India. Their wonderfully firm texture contrasts delightfully with soft, fluffy rice, and they provide an excellent boost of protein. In India, we would eat this pilau at lunchtime, but at home I serve it in the evening to make the most of the full, sleepy feeling we all get from eating lots of rice. It is great with a curry that has plenty of sauce, so it can soak up all those lovely flavours.

SERVES 4

Masala
4–6 fresh green chillies (ideally Kenyan)
5 cloves of garlic, soaked and peeled
4cm root ginger, peeled
pinch of salt

50ml sunflower oil
1 tsp cumin seeds
200g frozen pigeon peas, thawed
1¼ tsp salt
½ tsp turmeric
200g basmati rice, gently washed and drained twice
45g butter
500ml water

Crush the chillies, garlic and ginger together with a pinch of salt using a pestle and mortar (or a blender), to make a fine masala paste.

Heat the oil in a thick-based pan for 1½ minutes. Add the cumin seeds and swirl through the oil for 30 seconds, then add the pigeon peas, masala paste, salt and turmeric and stir for 1 minute. Add the drained rice and enjoy the sizzle. Stir for 45 seconds, then add the butter and water and stir again. Half-cover with the lid and cook for 16 minutes, stirring through after 10 minutes.

Put a large square of aluminium foil on top of the rice and tuck it into the edges of the pan to seal the rice in and keep it moist and fluffy while it steams. Cover with the lid, reduce the heat to the lowest setting and cook for 9 minutes. Take off the heat and leave to rest covered for 5 minutes.

Serve hot with *tameta reveya* (page 45) or *bataka tameta* (page 47).

BAATH ᖳ boiled basmati rice

(V, WF, OG, N, HO)

Back in India, our families are farmers whose main crop is rice. This isn't surprising, given that the main part of any Gujarati meal will always be accompanied by a generous serving of rice. Basmati rice, with its long grains and delicate flavour, tends to be less starchy than shorter-grained rice. It also has a sweet fragrance, which gives it its name – basmati means 'full of aroma' in Hindi. I always use Tilda basmati rice because I find that it has the best taste and texture.

SERVES 4

300g basmati rice
40ml sunflower oil
½ tsp salt
900ml boiling water

Rinse the rice in warm water, running your fingers gently through it before draining, then repeat. Washing it twice removes enough starch to make the cooked rice fluffy and loose.

Heat the oil in a large pan over a medium heat for 30 seconds. Add the rice and gently stir through to coat in oil, then add the salt and boiling water. Using boiling water helps the rice to cook quickly initially, which makes a huge difference to the texture.

Boil the rice uncovered over a high heat for 10 minutes or so, stirring occasionally, until almost all the water has cooked off and the rice starts to look dry on top.

Put a large square of aluminium foil on top of the rice and tuck it into the edges of the pan to seal the rice in and keep it moist and fluffy while it steams. Cover with the lid, reduce the heat to the lowest setting and leave to cook for 5 minutes. Remove from the heat and set aside to rest covered for at least 5 minutes.

When you remove the foil, the rice should be standing on end and perfectly cooked. Gently run a spoon through it to loosen, taking care not to break the rice grains, then serve straight away. I love to just eat *baath* with other simple accompaniments like *dhal* (page 228) or *khudi* (page 226), but it goes with most dishes, so take your pick.

JEERA BAATH ⟨ cumin-infused rice

(V, WF, N, HO)

As an easy alternative to your usual plain rice, try this onion- and cumin-infused version. It has quite a bold flavour, so serve it with curries that have a stronger flavour profile. It's particularly good with spicy tomato-based Punjabi ones, such as rajma *(page 60), or my vine tomato satay (page 45).*

SERVES 4

300g basmati rice
75ml sunflower oil
1 tsp cumin seeds
1 medium onion, chopped in rings
1¼ tsp salt
900ml boiling water

Rinse the rice in warm water, running your fingers gently through it before draining, then repeat. Washing it twice removes enough starch to make the cooked rice fluffy and loose.

Heat the oil in a large pan for a minute over a medium heat before stirring in the cumin seeds. Keep an eye on them as they bubble in the oil and when they start to go brown, stir in the onion.

Increase the heat to high, cover the pan and leave the onion to cook gently for 2 minutes before stirring. Repeat the covered cooking and stirring several times, until the onion has caramelised to a lovely dark brown (this should take about 7–8 minutes). It is important to brown the onion like this, taking care not to burn it, as the more time you take at this stage to infuse it in the cumin oil, the richer the flavour and the deeper the colour of the finished dish.

Add the rice, gently stir through to coat, then add the salt and boiling water and gently stir to combine. Using boiling water helps the rice to cook quickly initially, which makes a huge difference to the texture. Boil uncovered for 6–7 minutes, stirring occasionally, until almost all the water has cooked off and the rice starts to look dry on top.

Put a large square of aluminium foil on top of the rice and tuck it into the edges of the pan to seal the rice in and keep it moist and fluffy while it steams. Cover with the lid, reduce the heat to the lowest setting and leave to cook for 6–7 minutes. Remove from the heat and set aside to rest covered for at least 5 minutes.

When you remove the foil, everything should be perfectly cooked. Gently run a spoon through it to loosen, taking care not to break the rice grains, then serve straight away with *paneer & mattar bhurgi* (page 56) and *tameta reveya* (page 45).

TUVAR DHAL KICHDI ~ pigeon peas and rice

(V (optional), WF, OG, N, HO)

Protein-rich tuvar or toor dhal is made from hulled split pigeon peas, which have been grown in India for more than 3,000 years. I love to think of all the generations before me who have made versions of this dish. There are lots of different recipes around, but I like to keep things very simple and use just a combination of butter and turmeric to add flavour. Whenever my husband is travelling back from a business trip, I can guarantee that he will be thinking about enjoying this on his return home. I like to use Malawian tuvar dhal because it has a great depth of flavour and is easy to cook.

SERVES 4

150g *tuvar dhal* (dried pigeon
  peas / yellow lentils)
200g basmati rice
75ml sunflower oil
1¼ tsp salt
½ tsp turmeric
925ml boiling water
45g butter (optional)

Rinse the *tuvar dhal* at least three times in hot water, using your fingers to rub the oily coating away and check for small stones, then leave to soak in hot water for at least 10 minutes before draining. Rinse the rice in warm water, running your fingers gently through it before draining, then repeat. Washing it twice removes enough starch to make the cooked rice fluffy and loose.

Heat the oil in a large pan for a minute over a medium heat. Add the *dhal* and rice and fry together for a minute, gently stirring to coat them in oil. Stir in the salt, turmeric and boiling water – it is essential that the water is boiling, as it helps the rice to cook quickly initially, which makes a great difference to the texture.

Bring to the boil, then simmer uncovered over a medium heat for 10–12 minutes, until the majority of the water has cooked off and the *dhal*-rice mixture starts to look dry on top. Then reduce the heat to its lowest setting and stir in the butter (if using). Put a large square of aluminium foil on top of the rice and *dhal*, tucking it into the edges of the pan to seal everything in and keep the rice moist and fluffy while it steams. Cover with the lid, reduce the heat to the lowest setting and leave to cook for 6–7 minutes. Remove from the heat and set aside to rest for at least 5 minutes.

Stir through gently with a spoon to loosen any clumps – use a light touch or you risk breaking the rice grains, ruining your hard work. Serve immediately with *lasan bhaji* (page 55) or *khanda bataka* (page 48).

PALAK PURI ⟨ spinach 'clouds'

(N)

Puri are traditionally served at lavish Indian weddings, either cooked the day before and eaten cold, or fried on the day and served piping hot. The secret to making great puri lies in kneading the dough thoroughly, and then frying it at the correct temperature. If you get these two right, your puri should be wonderfully light and flaky – one of our customers described them as little clouds floating to the table, so that's what we call them on our menu. This spinach-infused version of the ones we serve in the restaurant is extra-special. Drying the spinach overnight avoids putting excess moisture into the dough, which may prevent the puri from being light and flaky.

MAKES 15-20 MINI PURI

Masala
3 fresh green chillies (ideally Kenyan)
2 cloves of garlic, soaked and peeled
pinch of salt

1½ tsp cumin seeds
1 bunch of spinach (approx. 150g), washed and left out to dry overnight
300g chapatti flour, sieved, plus extra for dusting
100ml water
25g fine semolina
1¼ tsp salt
30ml sunflower oil, plus more for frying

Crush the chillies and garlic together with a pinch of salt using a pestle and mortar (or a blender), to make a fine masala paste.

Toast the cumin seeds in a dry frying pan for 30 seconds, then swirl them around the pan and toast for another 30 seconds before taking off the heat. Crush using a rolling pin or pestle and mortar, and set aside.

Chop the dried spinach to a fine pulp using a blender. You will need to stop and push the spinach down into the blender a few times to ensure that it all gets fully blitzed. Mix the spinach pulp with the masala paste in a large bowl. Add the toasted ground cumin, flour, water, semolina, salt and oil and knead the dough until all the ingredients are well mixed. Taste and season if needed.

Divide the dough into 19 or 20 pieces of about 33g each. Very lightly dust your worktop with a small amount of flour – just enough to prevent sticking (be conservative). Smooth each piece of dough into a ball in palm of your hand and squeeze slightly to flatten it before rolling into a disc approximately 11cm in diameter. Place each *puri* on a separate sheet of greaseproof paper.

Heat the frying oil – about 10cm deep – in a large pan over a high heat (or in a deep fat fryer, if you

CONTINUED OVERLEAF

have one) and when you think it is hot enough, test the temperature by dropping a little of the dough into the oil. When it is up to temperature, the pieces will quickly spring back up to float on the surface. Reduce the heat to medium.

Gently place a couple of *puri* in the oil. As soon as they puff up, use a heatproof spoon or ladle to turn them, then spoon oil over them to help them cook evenly. Fry for 1–2 minutes until golden brown and puffed full of air. Remove from the oil with a slotted spoon or strainer and leave to rest on absorbent kitchen towel while you fry the next batch. Repeat until all the *puri* have been fried.

Serve hot or cold (I think they are best eaten hot and crispy straight from the pan). *Puri* goes particularly well with rich tomato-based dishes like *sabzi & paneer makni* (page 101) or *soya & wattana keema* (page 63). Any left over can be stored in an airtight container once they've cooled and eaten cold the next day with curry, or with plain natural yoghurt and a cup of *masala chai* (page 247).

KAKRA BHAJIA ⟨ paprika potato crisps

(V, WF, OG, N, HO)

Gujaratis love to snack and my family is no exception. These crunchy crisps are great for dipping into some kopru *(page 235) or* imli *chutney (page 241). They also make a great accompaniment to the* paneer tikka *(page 69), providing a lovely contrast of textures. The thinner you make the potato slices, the crunchier and tastier they'll be.*

SERVES 4

100g gram (chickpea) flour, sieved

100g rice flour, sieved

1¼ tsp salt

1 tsp ground coriander

¼ tsp ground cumin

1 tsp carom seeds

pinch turmeric

2 medium red-skinned (or other waxy) potatoes (approx. 300g), peeled and sliced in thin discs using a sharp knife or a mandolin on the thinnest setting

sunflower oil for deep-frying

1 tsp medium red chilli powder

Mix the gram flour, rice flour, salt, coriander, cumin, carom seeds and turmeric together in a large bowl and tip into a shallow tray. Spread about 20 potato slices on top of the flour mixture and shake the tray to coat them. Don't worry if the slices aren't completely floured as long as they have a pretty good coating.

Heat the frying oil – about 10cm deep – in a large pan over a high heat (or in a deep fat fryer, if you have one). Drop one floured potato slice into the oil and when it starts bubbling, reduce to medium heat and add as many as will comfortably fit in the pan at a time. Fry for 1–2 minutes, stirring with a wooden or heatproof plastic spoon until crispy and golden brown, then remove from the oil with a slotted spoon and place on absorbent kitchen towel for 10 seconds before sprinkling with the chilli powder. Repeat with the rest of the potato slices.

Serve with *imli chutney* (page 241), either on their own as a little snack or to accompany *paneer tikka* (page 69).

BHINDA FRIES ୧ crispy okra chips

(V, WF, N)

Perfected by one of my sons, Mayur, to serve at his bar, Bundobust, in Leeds, these tasty chips are so popular that his okra supplier has found it hard to keep up with demand and has had to look elsewhere for additional sources! Okra can sometimes be a bit gluey, which can put people off, but it is a truly fantastic Indian vegetable that soaks up spices beautifully. Drying the okra in advance of frying helps the chips become really crispy. They are easy to make and are great as a snack on their own or as an accompaniment to almost anything, from Hyderabadi biryani *(page 191) to a speedy* Mumbai sandwich *(page 40). And I'm told they also go really well with a pint of coriander Pilsner! (Which was made exclusively as a house beer for Bundobust.) The* chaat masala *is really important to the flavours in this dish: it's the magical mixture of spices and salt that makes them so moreish.*

SERVES 4

2 tsp *chaat masala*
2 tsp medium red chilli powder
1 tsp turmeric
2 tsp ground coriander
¼ tsp ground cumin
½ tsp salt
sunflower oil for deep-frying
600g okra, topped, tailed, cut in
  half and left out to dry for 3 hours

Mix the *chaat masala*, chilli powder, turmeric, ground coriander, ground cumin and salt in a bowl.

Heat the frying oil – about 10cm deep – in a large pan over a high heat (or in a deep fat fryer, if you have one). Drop one piece of okra into the oil and when it starts bubbling, reduce to a medium heat and put in as many okra pieces as will comfortably fit in the pan. Fry the okra for 5 minutes, then remove from the oil with a slotted spoon and place on absorbent kitchen towel for 10 seconds to drain. Put in a bowl and sprinkle with some of the spice mix. Repeat with the rest of the okra until it has all been fried and seasoned. Enjoy straight away.

MASALA CHIPS (v, wf, n)

When Minal lived in India, this was the style of chips she would enjoy snacking on when she was out with friends in Bardoli. They are a popular street food and once you've tasted them, you'll see why. Minal made them for us on one of her days off, and they were an instant hit. In fact, they tasted so good that we started serving them in the restaurant. I like to serve them with shimla makai *(page 59) and spicy pea and potato pasties (page 140).*

SERVES 4

Masala
3–5 fresh green chillies (ideally Kenyan)
4–6 cloves of garlic, soaked and peeled
pinch of salt

25ml sunflower oil, plus more for deep-frying
3 large red-skinned (or other waxy) potatoes (approx. 950g), peeled, chopped into thick chips and soaked in ice-cold water for 1 hour
1 tsp salt
1 tsp pepper
juice of ½ lime

Crush the chillies and garlic together with a pinch of salt using a pestle and mortar (or a blender), to make a fine masala paste.

Heat 25ml of sunflower oil in a large frying pan on a medium heat for 45 seconds, then turn to a low heat. Add the masala paste and stir and fry for 1 minute. Take off the heat.

Take the potatoes out of the cold water and drain thoroughly. Heat the frying oil – about 10cm deep – in a large pan over a high heat (or in a deep fat fryer, if you have one). Drop one chip into the oil and when it starts bubbling, reduce to a medium heat and add as many as will comfortably fit in the pan at a time. Fry until crispy, then remove from the oil with a slotted spoon and place on absorbent kitchen towel for 10 seconds.

Tip the chips into a bowl, toss with the masala paste, season with the salt, pepper and lime juice, then tuck in.

STICKY CHILLI CHIPS (V, WF, N)

It used to make me laugh when people came into the restaurant and ordered a selection of elaborate, Indian dishes full of complex spices and flavourings, and then sheepishly asked for a portion of chips on the side! I don't care though; I love a bit of combining of cultures. This is my Gujarati take on the humble potato chip, coated in a wonderfully sticky, slightly spiced sauce.

SERVES 4

3 large red-skinned (or other waxy) potatoes (approx. 950g), peeled, chopped into thick chips and soaked in ice-cold water for 1 hour
sunflower oil for deep-frying
50g tomato ketchup
20g *lasan* chutney (page 239)
1 tsp salt

Take the potatoes out of the cold water and drain thoroughly. Heat the frying oil – about 10cm deep – in a large pan over a high heat (or in a deep fat fryer, if you have one). Drop one chip into the oil and when it starts bubbling, reduce to medium heat add as many as will comfortably fit in the pan at a time. Fry until crispy then remove from the oil with a slotted spoon and place on absorbent kitchen towel for 10 seconds. Tip the chips into a bowl and toss with the ketchup, *lasan* chutney and salt.

Serve immediately with spicy veggie burgers (page 139) or Indo-Italian macaroni cheese (page 143).

KHUDI ∙ spiced yoghurt soup

(WF, OG, N, HO)

In India, my grandmother kept fifteen cows and buffalo, meaning that many of the dishes she cooked were based around yoghurt or other dairy products. This light, tangy sauce (also known as kadhi *or* karhi*) is best served with rice dishes, such as* baath *(page 213) or* tuvar dhal kichdi *(page 217). Fresh turmeric and white turmeric root can be used much like root ginger in cooking, but white turmeric can be a bit harder to find, as it is very seasonal. Don't worry if you can't get hold of any; just leave it out, as there'll be plenty of flavour from the other spices. When buying fresh turmeric of either kind, look for roots that are firm to the touch – the older they get, the softer they become. In Gujarati cooking we use a special mini frying pan called a* vagariu *or* bhagar *pan especially for preparing spiced oils, but you can use any small frying pan.*

SERVES 4

Masala
1 fresh green chilli (ideally Kenyan),
 trimmed but not de-seeded
1cm turmeric root, peeled and
 roughly chopped
8cm white turmeric root (*amba
 haldi*), peeled and roughly chopped
6 fresh curry leaves, washed
1 handful fresh coriander, washed
 and finely chopped
¼ tsp cumin seeds

425g plain live set yoghurt
1 tbsp gram (chickpea) flour, sieved
500ml cold water
1¼ tsp salt
1 tbsp sugar

Tarka (spiced oil)
50ml sunflower oil
1 dried red chilli, snapped in half
1 tsp cumin seeds
1 tsp brown mustard seeds
10 fresh curry leaves, washed
1 handful fresh coriander,
 washed and finely chopped

Crush the chilli, turmeric, white turmeric, curry leaves, fresh coriander and cumin seeds together with a pestle and mortar (or in a blender) to make a fine masala paste.

Whisk the yoghurt and gram flour together in a large pan to combine, then add the water and whisk (or blitz with a handheld blender) until smooth. Place over a medium heat and stir in the masala paste, salt and sugar. Cook for 4–5 minutes, stirring continuously to ensure that the yoghurt doesn't split, then remove from the heat.

Heat the oil in a small pan or frying pan for 30 seconds over a medium heat, then add the red chilli. Once it starts to turn darker (after about 30 seconds), add the cumin and mustard seeds. As soon as the mustard seeds start to pop, add the curry leaves (be careful, as they will sizzle and spit) and then the coriander.

Slowly and carefully pour a ladleful of the yoghurt mixture into the *tarka*, a little at a time – I do this at arm's length, as the hot *tarka* will spit. Stir through, then pour the contents of the *tarka* pan into the large pan containing the rest of the yoghurt mixture and stir to combine.

Stir through, then remove from the heat and leave to rest covered for at least 10 minutes. Once cooled, store in the fridge until needed (I prepare it up to 5 hours in advance of eating).

When you are ready to eat, gently reheat the *khudi* over a medium heat, stirring occasionally, and bring to the boil before serving. Be careful not to leave it cooking for too long, as the longer you heat it, the thicker it becomes.

Khudi goes wonderfully with *mung dhal* (page 73), *lasan bhaji* (page 55), or *tuvar dhal kichdi* (page 217). Any leftover *khudi* can be stored in an airtight container in the fridge for a day or two. It gets thicker each time it's heated, so add a dash of water to bring it back to its original consistency when reheating.

DHAL ⟨ traditional yellow lentil soup

(V, WF, OG, N, HO)

This sweet, spicy dhal *makes a wonderfully rich sauce to accompany* baath *(page 213), but it can also be eaten on its own as a light meal. Dinnertimes around an Indian table are all about combining the flavours and textures of the different dishes to fully appreciate their complexity, so there's usually a lot of noisy eating as we mix-and-match the food on our plates. I love nothing more than to hear my family slurping away – it shows they are really enjoying my cooking!*

SERVES 4

200g *tuvar dhal* (dried pigeon
  peas / yellow lentils)
3 ltr boiling water
1 tsp sunflower oil
1 x 400g tin peeled plum tomatoes,
  finely chopped or blended
4cm root ginger, peeled and roughly
  chopped
2 tsp salt
1 tsp turmeric
1 tsp medium red chilli powder
60 g *jaggery*, cut in thin flakes
  (or demerara / soft brown sugar)
1 handful fresh coriander, washed
  and finely chopped

Tarka (spiced oil)
50ml sunflower oil
2 dried red chillies, snapped in half
1 tsp cumin seeds
1 tsp brown mustard seeds
¼ tsp asafetida

Rinse the *tuvar dhal* at least four times in hot water, using your fingertips to rub the oily coating away and check for any small stones. Leave to soak in hot water for 15 minutes to soften, then drain.

Put the *dhal* in a large pan with 2 litres of the boiling water (you can add most of the water now and the remainder once some has cooked off if your pan isn't big enough to take it all at once). Bring to the boil, then simmer over a medium heat for a couple of minutes until it starts to foam. Skim the froth from the surface, add the teaspoon of oil and simmer three-quarters covered for about 25 minutes, stirring occasionally, until the *dhal* is cooked through (it should squash easily between your thumb and forefinger).

Add the tomatoes and the remaining litre of boiling water. Bring the mixture back to the boil, then simmer three-quarters covered over a medium heat for 3–4 minutes.

Remove from the heat and blitz with a blender until the mixture has a really smooth texture, using a spatula to scoop any unblitzed *dhal* from the sides of the pan. Return to a medium heat and simmer gently uncovered while you prepare the spices and seasoning.

Crush the ginger with a pestle and mortar (or in a blender) to make a fine pulp. Add the crushed ginger, salt, turmeric, chilli powder, *jaggery* and chopped coriander to the *dhal* mixture and stir through.

Heat the sunflower oil for the *tarka* in a small pan over a medium heat for about 30 seconds before adding the red chillies and cumin seeds. When the cumin seeds start to turn darker brown (after about 30 seconds), add the mustard seeds. As soon as the mustard seeds start to pop, add the asafetida.

Slowly and carefully pour a ladleful of the *dhal* into the *tarka*, a little at a time – I do this at arm's length, as the hot *tarka* will spit. Stir through, then pour the contents of the *tarka* pan into the large pan containing the rest of the *dhal* mixture and stir to combine.

Bring the *dhal* back to the boil and simmer for 3–4 minutes before removing from the heat. Leave to rest covered for at least 20 minutes, to allow the flavours to develop.

Reheat to boiling before serving, stirring well to mix in the magic from the bottom of the pan. *Dhal* goes well with many dishes – I particularly like it with *sukhu parvar bataka* (page 82) or *sukhu kobi wattana* (page 57). If you have any left over, it can be stored in an airtight container in the fridge for a couple of days. When reheating, add a little water to loosen if you think it needs it.

SAMBAR & aromatic vegetable and lentil soup

(V, WF, OG, N, HO)

In the garden in India, my grandmother used to grow beautiful small aubergines, and I picture them whenever I make this soup. Sambar originally comes from southern India, but is now enjoyed by people the world over because it is light and healthy but full of the most amazing flavours. You can eat it on its own, or serve it with baath *(page 213) and* kopru *chutney (page 235). Sambar is a vital component in* idli sambar *(page 88) (the name is a clue!) and I also really enjoy it when paired with my* uttapam *vegetable pancakes (page 85).*

SERVES 4-6

200g *tuvar dhal* (split pigeon
   peas / yellow lentils)
2 ltr boiling water
1 tsp sunflower oil
1 x 400g tin peeled plum tomatoes,
   finely chopped or blended
1 baby aubergine, cut in 1cm cubes
1 small-medium bottle gourd,
   peeled and cut in 1cm cubes
4cm root ginger, peeled and roughly
   chopped
30g fresh or frozen peas (ideally
   petits pois)
2½ tsp salt
1 tsp turmeric
1 tsp medium red chilli powder
1 tbsp granulated sugar
½ tsp *garam masala*
1 handful fresh coriander, washed
   and finely chopped

Tarka (spiced oil)
50ml sunflower oil
1 tsp cumin seeds
1 tsp brown mustard seeds
¼ tsp asafetida
10 fresh curry leaves, washed

Rinse the *tuvar dhal* at least four times in hot water, using your fingertips to rub the oily coating away and check for small stones, then leave to soak in hot water for 15 minutes before draining.

Put the *dhal* in a large pan with 1.5 litres of boiling water (you can add one litre now and top up with the remainder while the *dhal* is cooking if your pan isn't big enough to take 1.5 litres all at once). Bring to the boil, then simmer over a medium heat for a couple of minutes until it starts to foam. Skim the froth from the surface, add the teaspoon of oil and simmer three-quarters covered for a further 28–30 minutes, stirring occasionally, until the *dhal* is cooked through (it should squash easily between your thumb and forefinger).

Add the tomatoes, bring the mixture back to the boil and simmer three-quarters covered again over a medium heat for 2–3 minutes, stirring every minute or so. Remove from the heat and blitz with a blender until the mixture has a really smooth texture.

Return the pan with the blended *dhal*-tomato mixture to a medium heat, stir in the aubergine and bottle gourd cubes along with the last 500ml of boiling water and leave to cook uncovered for 2–3 minutes. While it is cooking, crush the ginger

CONTINUED OVERLEAF

with a pestle and mortar (or in a blender) to make a fine pulp.

Add the ginger, peas, salt, turmeric, chilli powder, sugar, *garam masala* and chopped coriander to the *dhal* mixture and stir through. Leave to simmer gently uncovered for 4–5 minutes while you prepare the *tarka*.

Heat the sunflower oil in a small pan over a medium heat for about 30 seconds, then add the cumin seeds. When they start to darken (after about 30 seconds), tip in the mustard seeds, and as soon as they start to pop, add the asafetida. Add the curry leaves (be careful, as they will sizzle and spit), then slowly and carefully pour in a ladleful of the lentil-vegetable mixture, a little at a time – I do this at arm's length, as the hot *tarka* will spit. Stir through, then pour the contents of the small pan into the large pan containing the rest of the lentil mixture and stir again.

Bring the *sambar* to the boil and simmer for 10–12 minutes partially covered over a low heat, stirring occasionally. Remove from the heat, cover and leave to rest for 15 minutes to allow the flavours to develop.

Reheat to boiling before serving, making sure that you stir well, as some of the magic will be at the bottom of the pan. Any leftovers can be stored in an airtight container in the fridge for a couple of days, to be reheated with a little extra water and enjoyed as a speedy lunch or supper.

MITU GAJAR MURABHO ~ sweet carrot pickle

(V, WF, OG, N)

This variation on traditional sweet mango chutney is a joint invention with my daughter-in-law, Minal. I really like the simplicity of this pickle – it's quick and easy to prepare, plus you have the added advantage that you don't have to wait until mango season to make it. (See photograph on page 236.)

MAKES ABOUT 400ML

250g sugar
500g carrots, peeled and grated
6–8cm cinnamon stick
4 cardamom pods, split open
4 cloves
4–5 strips of saffron
½ tsp citric acid
50ml water

Preheat the oven to 100°C/80°C fan/gas mark ¼ while you wash a few glass jars, then pop them into the oven for 10 minutes to dry and sterilise them. Stand them upside down on a clean tea towel until you need them.

Put the sugar and carrots in a large thick-based pan on a medium heat and gently stir for 6–7 minutes. Stir in the cinnamon, cardamom pods, cloves, saffron, citric acid and water and lightly simmer for 11–12 minutes, stirring throughout. Take off the heat and set aside to cool completely.

Pour the cooled *murabho* into the sterilised glass jars, making sure the lids are firmly closed to ensure that they are airtight. This mouth-watering sweet pickle will keep for up to 2 months.

Serve with *Hyderabadi biryani* (page 191) or *Rajasthani gatta* (page 98).

KOPRU ⟨ mustard seed, curry leaf and coconut dip

(WF, OG, N, HO)

There's a curry leaf tree at my grandmother's house in India that is more than a hundred years old; more than five generations have been picking leaves from it and cooking with them. I made this dip to go with my South Indian dishes, although my version includes yoghurt, which is not strictly as it would be made in South India – you'll have realised by now, though, that I like to add my own twist to dishes! Make this before cooking the rest of your meal so that it has a good long time to chill in the fridge before serving. The chilling helps the flavours come together and helps keep the texture lovely and firm. (See photograph on page 236.)

SERVES 4-6

425g plain live set yoghurt

70g coarse unsweetened
  desiccated coconut

½ tsp salt

2 tsp granulated sugar

2 handfuls fresh coriander, washed
  and finely chopped

2 fresh green chillies (ideally
  Kenyan), trimmed but not
  de-seeded

75ml sunflower oil

1 tsp brown mustard seeds

1 tsp cumin seeds

10 fresh curry leaves, washed

Tip the yoghurt into a medium bowl and stir until smooth, then stir in the coconut, salt and sugar.

Blitz half the chopped coriander with the chillies in a blender to a medium coarse texture. Scoop into the yoghurt mixture and stir through.

Heat the oil in a small pan for a minute over a medium heat before adding the mustard seeds and cumin seeds. When the mustard seeds start to pop, add the curry leaves and the rest of the chopped coriander (be careful, as the leaves will sizzle and spit as they meet the oil) and stir through. Remove the pan from the heat.

Pour the spiced oil into the yoghurt mixture and stir to combine. Cover with cling film and store in the refrigerator until you are ready to serve, so that it will be lovely and cold when you come to eat it. This is traditionally served with *idli sambar* (page 88) or *uttapam* (page 85).

SHIMLA MIRCH ‹ red pepper and carrot relish

(V, WF, OG, N, HO)

This is a warming yet delicate relish that works well with starters. I always make some at Christmas when I want to add something red to our dishes. It will keep in an airtight container in the fridge for a couple of days. (See photograph opposite.)

SERVES 4-6

1 tsp cumin seeds
1 small carrot, peeled
  and cut in 6 pieces
1 clove of garlic
1 green chilli (ideally Kenyan),
  trimmed but not de-seeded
¾ tsp salt
2 tsp granulated sugar
1 medium red pepper, trimmed,
  de-seeded and cut in 8 pieces
4 tsp white vinegar

Dry-roast the cumin seeds in a frying pan over a low heat – gently shake the pan and when they start to turn dark brown, remove from the heat, tip into a small bowl and leave to cool for 3–5 minutes.

Blitz the carrot for a few seconds in a blender to break down to a coarse texture. Add the roasted cumin seeds and all the other ingredients and blitz again to a medium-coarse pulp. Pour into a small bowl and serve straight away, or cover and chill until needed.

This is a very versatile chutney that goes well with many dishes. I love to serve it with *palak & paneer googra* (page 126) and *sabudana vada* (page 116).

1. sweet and tangy tamarind chutney
2. apple and pea chutney
3. garlic and red chilli chutney
4. mustard seed, curry leaf and coconut dip
5. sweet carrot pickle
6. red pepper and carrot relish

SAFARJAN WATTANA ⋲ apple and pea chutney

(V, WF, N, HO)

From the very first day we opened Prashad, it was my aim to do things the way I do at home. 'Fresh and fantastic' is my mantra. This is reflected perfectly in this classic dip, which combines sweet garden peas and sour apple – two very English ingredients, prepared in a traditional Gujarati way. It goes down very well with our customers as an alternative to mango chutney for dipping their poppadoms. It will keep fresh for up to a week in an airtight jar in the fridge. (See photograph on page 236.)

MAKES ABOUT 400ML

100g garden peas (fresh or frozen)
½ large cooking apple,
　cored and cut in 1cm cubes
½ bunch fresh coriander, washed
　and trimmed of stalk ends
1 tbsp ground cumin
1 tsp salt
2½ tsp granulated sugar
1–2 fresh green chillies
　(ideally Kenyan), trimmed
　but not de-seeded
1–3 cloves garlic
30g *sev* (Indian vermicelli)
1 tbsp lemon juice

Preheat the oven to 100°C/80°C fan/gas mark ¼ while you wash a large glass jar, then pop it in the oven for 10 minutes to dry and sterilise it. Stand it upside down on a clean tea towel until needed.

Rinse the peas in warm water to start them thawing (if using frozen), then drain. Blitz the peas, apple and coriander to a medium coarse texture in a blender or food processor. Add the remaining ingredients and blitz together to a coarse, slightly runny texture.

Scoop into the sterilised glass jar, making sure that the lid is firmly closed to ensure that it is airtight. Store in the fridge until needed. This is ideal with *mausami tikki* (page 124) or *paneer* spheres (page 123).

LASAN CHUTNEY ❧ garlic and red chilli chutney

(V, WF, N, HO)

Lasan is a real gem of a chutney and is the finishing jewel in my streetside chaat *dishes. Use it to make my* sev momra bhel *(page 109), or whenever you feel in need of a garlicky chilli kick. And don't think that you can only use it with Indian food – used sparingly or in dilution, this flavoursome chutney is perfect for chilli-lovers to add a fiery boost to pizza toppings, or even to pep up sandwiches for packed lunches. (See photograph on page 236.)*

MAKES ABOUT 550ML

50g garlic (13–14 cloves)
100ml lemon juice
50g medium red chilli powder
2½ tsp salt
400ml cold water

Preheat the oven to 100°C/80°C fan/gas mark ¼ while you wash a couple of jam jars, then pop them in the oven for 10 minutes to dry and sterilise them. Stand them upside down on a clean tea towel until you need them.

Blitz the garlic in a blender until roughly chopped, then add the lemon juice and blitz again until you have a grainy pulp. Add the chilli powder, salt and half the water and blitz for a third time until the mixture is lovely and smooth.

Tip the chutney into a mixing bowl, making sure that you scoop every last drop out, then add the remaining water and stir gently to mix through.

Pour in to the sterilised glass jars, making sure that the lids are firmly closed to ensure that they are airtight. Stored in the fridge, this will keep for up to 6 weeks.

IMLI CHUTNEY ◊ sweet and tangy tamarind chutney

(V, WF, OG, N)

I used to love climbing trees as a child, much to my grandmother's annoyance, and there was a particular imli *tree in the back garden that was a favourite of mine. The views from the top were spectacular, and I used to pick the fruit while I was there. I had to be careful not to fall out, though, as there was a particularly vicious bed of nettles at the bottom! Until my first cookbook, the Prashad recipe for* imli *chutney was a closely guarded family secret, but I decided to share it with you, as it's just too good to miss – so use it wisely! To make a larger batch, just double the amounts below. It is a key component in* sev momra bhel *(page 109) and* dabeli *(page 112), and goes brilliantly with* chaat, bhel *and* bhaji *dishes generally. (See photograph on page 236.)*

MAKES ABOUT 400ML

100g dried tamarind (from a block),
  broken in 4cm square pieces
75g stoned dates, broken in
  large chunks (roughly 2cm long)
50g *jaggery*, cut in thin flakes (or
  demerara / soft brown sugar)
50g granulated sugar
1.5 ltr boiling water
¾ tsp salt
1 tsp medium red chilli powder
1 tsp ground cumin
cold water to dilute

Preheat the oven to 100°C/80°C fan/gas mark ¼ while you wash a couple of glass jars, then pop them in the oven for 10 minutes to dry and sterilise them. Stand them upside down on a clean tea towel until you need them.

Put the tamarind, dates, *jaggery* and sugar in a large pan. Pour in the boiling water and cook over a high heat for 25 minutes. Stir frequently and scrape down the sides to make nothing scorches or burns. Once the mixture has reduced down to a thick flavoursome sauce, remove from the heat and set aside to cool, stirring occasionally. This can take up to 2 hours, but you can halve this by setting the pan in a sinkful of cold water and stirring frequently to aid the cooling process.

Sieve the cooled chutney into a large bowl. Add the salt, chilli powder and cumin and blitz with a blender (or whisk). Then stir cold water through until you reach your preferred texture and thickness – 60ml will make it very slightly runny, which is how I like my *imli* chutney, but you may prefer to use more or less than this.

Pour into the sterilised glass jars, making sure that the lids are firmly closed to ensure that they are airtight. Store in the fridge for up to 3 weeks.

BARELA MARCHA ~ chillies with sweet cumin satay

(V, WF, OG)

As you've probably guessed, I love fresh chillies and sweet food. Mixing chillies with jaggery in this satay-style nutty dish is an instant way to satisfy any cravings I may have. Bullet chillies are small and green and they are less fiery than many other chillies, once you've removed the seeds. It is their milder heat and ability to absorb the sweetness from the jaggery that makes them perfect for this recipe. These sweet and spicy chillies are a fantastic warming accompaniment to almost anything in this book, but they are also great in a cheese sandwich: squish them into the bread, and lay the cheese on top. It's definitely a 'big boy' sandwich though – not one for the kids!

MAKES 16 STUFFED CHILLIES

100ml sunflower oil

200g red-skinned peanuts, coarsely blended

1 tsp cumin seeds

2 tsp salt

65g *jaggery*, finely flaked (or demerara / soft brown sugar)

15g sesame seeds

¼ tsp turmeric

4 tsp ground coriander

½ tsp ground cumin

16 bullet chillies, washed, carefully sliced down one side and de-seeded (stem kept on)

Mix the sunflower oil, ground peanuts, cumin seeds, salt, *jaggery*, sesame seeds, turmeric, ground coriander and ground cumin in a large bowl, rubbing through with your fingers and thumb and making sure the *jaggery* breaks down to create a sticky paste.

Make sure you have removed all the seeds from the chillies before starting otherwise they will be far too hot. Fill each chilli with plenty of paste, making sure that you get right into the ends. Be careful not to split them. Place each filled chilli open-side-up in a large non-stick frying pan. Scrape any excess paste from the bowl into the frying pan. Make sure that no flavour is wasted by washing out the bowl with 100ml of water (rinse any paste off your hands at the same time) and pour that into the pan as well.

Cover the pan with a lid and cook on a low heat for 11 minutes. Gently turn the chillies over, then re-cover and cook for another 5 minutes. Take off the heat, scrape everything out of the pan into a bowl and leave to rest for 10 minutes.

Store in an airtight container in the fridge for up to 3 weeks. I love to serve these with *sakabhaji upma* (page 42) or *pav vada* (page 114).

CHANA CHAAT PATTI ~ tangy chickpea salsa

(WF, N, HO)

You can serve this quick and easy salsa alongside pretty much any light lunch or supper dish to add another dimension to your meal. I particularly like it with sabudana kichdi *(page 41) or* tuvar dhokri vada *(page 120). It's good with leftovers too.*

SERVES 4-6

2 x 400g tins chickpeas
  (460g drained weight)
1 ltr boiling water
2 tsp cumin seeds
950g plain live set yoghurt
½ tsp salt
6 tsp sugar
100ml cold water
1 handful fresh coriander,
  washed and finely chopped
1 medium onion, finely chopped
1 tsp medium red chilli powder

Put the drained chickpeas in a large pan with the boiling water and cook uncovered for 4 minutes to soften them. Remove from the heat and drain.

Dry roast the cumin seeds in a small frying pan for 4 minutes on a low heat, swirling occasionally. Remove from the pan and grind the seeds using a pestle and mortar. Alternatively, you can place them on the worktop and roll a rolling pin, bottle or large glass over them until they are crushed.

Stir the set yoghurt in a bowl until smooth, then add the ground cumin seeds, salt and sugar and mix together well. Pour the cold water into the empty yoghurt containers and rinse them into the bowl to minimise waste. Mix in the chickpeas and half the fresh coriander.

Spread the mixture on a serving plate, cover and leave in the fridge for at least 10 minutes to chill. Just before serving, sprinkle with the chopped onion, chilli powder and remaining fresh coriander. This tastes best eaten on the day you make it.

MASALA CHAI & spicy tea

(WF, OG, N)

Just like the good old English cup of tea, chai is at the heart and hearth of every Indian home. Each household will have its own way of making it, but the pleasure felt when drinking this soothing, spicy tea will be much the same. In India the cups of tea are much smaller than in the UK, but they are drunk much more often and will be served with most snacks. I think this tea is best drunk with lots of sugar, but then I do have the traditional Gujarati sweet tooth.

SERVES 4

4 cardamom pods
3cm fresh cinnamon
4 black peppercorns
800ml water
5–6 tsp black tea leaves
65g sugar, plus more to taste
600ml whole milk

Heat the cardamom pods, cinnamon, peppercorns and water in a large pan over a high heat until the water comes to the boil, then stir in the tea leaves and sugar. Bring back to the boil and simmer for 2 minutes to allow the flavours to combine and work their magic.

Pour in the milk and simmer for 3 minutes over a high heat, stirring occasionally. Keep an eye on the pan and watch for bubbles forming around the edges (after about 2–3 minutes) – the milky tea can very quickly boil over if you're not careful. The moment it starts to foam up, remove from the heat and blow gently on the surface to cool the tea slightly until it sinks back down.

Reduce the heat to low, return the pan to the heat and leave to simmer for 5 minutes, stirring occasionally. If it stops simmering, briefly increase the heat to bring it back to the boil, then reduce the heat to low again.

Remove from the heat and pour through a tea strainer (or a clean sieve) into cups or mugs. Serve steaming hot, with extra sugar to add to taste.

KAUSHY'S
STORE CUPBOARD
AND
SUPPLIES

I am very lucky that I can buy all my fresh Indian vegetables, spices and supplies in local supermarkets in Bradford. If you have an Indian store nearby, ask them to help you with sourcing ingredients (and maybe a traditional *masala dabba* spice tin) – even if they don't sell what you're looking for, they should know where you can get hold of it. Many supermarkets now stock a good range of Indian food products and there are plenty of online suppliers too, such as www.itadka.com, www.spicesofindia.co.uk, www.asiangrocersonline.co.uk, www.theasiancookshop.co.uk and www.indianmart.co.uk, so between the high street and the internet you should be able to find what you need.

TO HELP YOU ACHIEVE THAT AUTHENTIC PRASHAD FLAVOUR, HERE ARE SOME OF MY FAVOURITE BRANDS:

ANCHOR unsalted butter
ASLI *atta* medium chapatti flour
COFRESH
 sev
 sev momra/mamra
DESI *paneer*
EAST END
 almonds, cashews and
  pistachios
 chana dhal/dal
 green cardamom pods
 mung dhal/dal
 resham patti and medium red
  chilli powder
 sesame seeds
 tinned chickpeas in brine
 urad dhal/urid dal
ENO fruit salts
FRESHONA (Lidl's own brand)
 tinned sweetcorn
GITS rice *idli* mix
HEERA (www.heeraspices.com)
 lemon juice
 cooking salt
HEINZ white vinegar
KHOLAPURI *jaggery*
LAKES pure butter *ghee*
JAIPUR sorghum flour

MDH
 Spices
 chunky *chat masala*
 pav bhaji masala
MAGGI hot red chilli sauce
MITCHELL'S green chilli sauce
MORRISONS cornflour
NAPOLINA tinned peeled
 plum tomatoes
NATCO
 fenugreek seeds and dried
  fenugreek leaves
 pauwa flattened rice
 red chillies, dried
 semolina, fine and coarse
 tamarind slab
 white poppy seeds
PAKEEZA live set natural yoghurt
PAPA *gram* (chickpea) flour
PEACOCK
 agar agar
 rice flour
PRIDE sunflower oil
SUGAM *paneer*
TATE & LYLE granulated sugar
TILDA basmati rice
TRS MALAWI *tuvar/toor dhal*
VANDEVI asafetida

ACKNOWLEDGEMENTS

Sri Guru Dev Dutt

Dada Bhagwan *na aseem jai jaikar ho*

Paying homage to Simandhar Swami and all my deities, I would like to say thank you to my dear, late mum, Santabha, for bringing me into this world, and to Prem Ma, my grandma, for sharing her love of food with me, enabling me to communicate our beautiful culture and cuisine through my books. Thank you to Laddubha, my late mother-in-law, for enjoying my food and complimenting me on my cooking.

Thank you to my husband Mohan, who is always there for me, always busy making sure I am OK. He is my rock and with him I feel I can do anything. We are really proud of our culture and cuisine, and together we hope we have inspired our children.

I would like to thank my customers for buying and using my first book. Your amazing feedback is the subject of many mealtime conversations in our home, and seeing pictures of my dishes on your dinner table is truly satisfying. I love that you really enjoy my food and I hope this book takes you on another culinary journey.

A big thank you to my son Bobby for giving me the courage and support to write this second book. In spite of running a very busy restaurant, he found time to work through every recipe and make sure that each one was accurately written down.

I would like to thank Minal, my daughter-in-law and head chef at Prashad, for encouraging me, sharing recipes, and making sure that this book has great balance. Her fusion dishes are amazing. She has a bright future ahead of her and I am right behind her.

Thank you to my granddaughter Maitri. Her interest in food at three years old is brilliant and I am excited to know that she will one day use my recipes too. When she bounds in from nursery shouting 'Bha bha', her energy lifts my fatigue after a hard day in the kitchen and gives me a fresh burst of life.

Thank you to Bhavesh, my son-in-law, for always wolfing down everything I cook, even when he is missing a certain ingredient. His appreciation is pure and I take great delight in feeding him.

I would like to thank my daughter Hina for inspiring some of my fusion dishes. As a child wanting a change from everyday Gujarati food, she encouraged me to think about my cooking and to work out how I could satisfy her sense of adventure.

Thank you to my darling grandson Tristan for working through his challenges and appreciating food. I know he loves my aubergine curry and I hope to cook it for him soon.

Thank you to my son Mayur for his ongoing passion for food. His creativity is boundless, and sharing some of the key recipes with him has been really helpful. I am happy to know that he is looking forward to using my new book, and who knows, we may even see some of my dishes on the Bundobust menu.

I would like to thank my future daughter-in-law Lucy for coming into our lives and bringing a special warmth. She has a wonderful, caring nature and it thrills me that she loves to eat my cooking.

I really enjoyed my time in India, which brought back memories of my childhood. Thank you to Prabha, my sister, for hosting us and not letting me miss my mum. My support team in India was truly great: Pratik, Ramesh and Mehul made sure we captured everything and got all that we needed. Living at home meant that we were able to pick fresh vegetables from the garden when cooking, just as I did during my childhood with Prem Ma.

Matt Russell has captured my world amazingly and I am really grateful to him. I take huge pleasure in gazing at the photos in this book.

Thank you to Helen Gill for helping Bobby get the manuscript ready. I know he really appreciated her involvement and efficiency.

Thank you to the publishing team, Elizabeth, Bryony, Kate and Laura, for the warm helping hand in making sure that the quality of this book is phenomenal. Many thanks for all the support and experience.

I had a lovely time in London on the photo shoot and would like to thank everyone who was there. It was amazing and very satisfying to see my recipes being cooked, and I still remember everyone laughing and enjoying my ginger tea.

In short, thank you to everyone who has helped me write this book. My family is like my right hand. They have embraced the challenge with me and helped me stay in the right frame of mind to produce my best recipes. Without them this book would not have been possible.

I hope you get as much joy from reading and using this book as I have from writing it. Remember: 'your mood decides your food', so cook what feels right for the occasion. Choose a recipe, enjoy the cooking process and make my food your own.

INDEX

Photographs for recipes are indicated by **bold** page references

A

agar agar 15
almonds: spiced nut parcels 192–3
amli see tamarind
angur rabri 196–7
apples:
    apple and pea chutney **236**, 238
    Indian fruit salad **194**, 195
arhar dhal 22
asafetida/asafoetida 7
asparagus:
    Indo-Chinese fried rice 157
    layered vegetable rice 188–9
    leek, broccoli, spinach and asparagus croquettes 124
    spicy veggie pie 141
    vegetable rice with mint masala **190**, 191
atta 16
aubergines 28
    aromatic vegetable and lentil soup 230, **231**, 232
    Gujarati mixed vegetable pot 182, **183**
    Indo-Italian veggie lasagne 144
    smoky mashed aubergine curry 86
    spicy fried aubergines 34, **35**
    vegetable rice with mint masala **190**, 191

B

baath 213
baked beans 136
bananas:
    Gujarati mixed vegetable pot 182, **183**
    Indian fruit salad **194**, 195
barela marcha **242**, 243
bataka chevda 174–5
bataka tameta 47
bathura 204–5, 208–9
bay leaves 12

bay leaf-infused new potato curry 90
beans 17
    black-eyed bean curry 62
    curried baked beans 136
    green *mung* bean curry 73
    Gujarati mixed vegetable pot 182, **183**
    hot and spicy stir-fry soup 160
    Indo-Chinese fried rice 157
    Indo-Mexican veggie enchiladas 161
    layered vegetable rice 188–9
    Punjabi-style kidney bean curry 60, **61**
    spiced sprouted *mung* beans 78, **79**
    spicy veggie pie 141
    tomato, carom and French bean curry 50, **51**
    vegetable *korma* 89
    vegetable rice with mint masala **190**, 191
    see also chickpeas; lentils; pigeon peas
besan see gram flour
bhagat muthia 96–7
bhajis:
    green pigeon pea and gram flour *bhajis* 120–1
    semolina-encrusted sweetcorn *bhajis* 118, **119**
    sweetcorn and onion *bhajis* 117
    tapioca, peanut and potato *bhajis* 116
bhakar vadi 180–1
bhakri: *methi bhakri* 203, **204–5**
bhel 153, **154**, 155
bhinda see okra
biryani:
    dum biryani 188–9
    Hyderabadi *biryani* **190**, 191
biscuits: crisp sugar biscuits 179
bitter melon/gourd 15
    stuffed bitter melon satay 80–1
black beans: Indo-Mexican veggie enchiladas 161
black-eyed bean curry 62

Bombay mix 174–5
bottle gourd 15
    aromatic vegetable and lentil soup 230, **231**, 232
    bottle gourd and coriander dumplings 52–3
bread:
    Indian fried bread 27, 111
    spicy bread and potato patties 114
    spicy mushroom and pepper pizza 150–1
    spinach 'clouds' **218**, 219–20
    see also buns; flatbreads; sandwiches
bread bhajia 27, 111
broad beans 17
    Gujarati mixed vegetable pot 182, **183**
broccoli:
    Indo-Chinese fried rice 157
    Indo-Chinese street food noodles 156
    layered vegetable rice 188–9
    leek, broccoli, spinach and asparagus croquettes 124
    mixed vegetable soup 37
    spicy veggie pie 141
    vegetable rice with mint masala **190**, 191
buns: mashed vegetable curry rolls 68
burgers: spicy veggie burgers **138**, 139

C

cabbage:
    cabbage pancakes 36
    cabbage and pea curry 57
    hot and spicy stir-fry soup 160
    Indo-Chinese street food noodles 156
    Indo-Chinese street-style rice and noodles 153, **154**, 155
    Manchurian cabbage dough balls with vegetable stir-fry 158–9, **159**
    vegetable patties in coriander, garlic and tomato

sauce 184–5
calabash *see* bottle gourd
cannelloni: Indo-Italian veggie
      cannelloni 144
cardamom 7, 27
      sweet cardamom vermicelli
            197
carom 7
      tomato, carom and French
            bean curry 50, **51**
carrots:
      hot and spicy stir-fry soup
            160
      Indo-Chinese fried rice 157
      Indo-Chinese street food
            noodles 156
      Indo-Chinese street-style rice
            and noodles 153,
            154, 155
      Indo-Italian macaroni cheese
            142, 143
      layered vegetable rice 188–9
      Manchurian cabbage dough
            balls with vegetable
            stir-fry 158–9, **159**
      mashed vegetable curry rolls
            68
      mixed vegetable soup 37
      red pepper and carrot relish
            236, 237
      savoury Indian porridge 42,
            43
      spicy veggie burgers **138**,
            139
      spicy veggie pie 141
      sweet carrot pickle 233, **236**
      vegetable *korma* 89
      vegetable patties in
            coriander, garlic and
            tomato sauce 184–5
      vegetable rice with mint
            masala **190**, 191
cashew nuts: Kaushy's Bombay
      mix 174–5
cauliflower:
      layered vegetable rice 188–9
      mashed vegetable curry rolls
            68
      vegetable *korma* 89
      vegetable patties in
            coriander, garlic and
            tomato sauce 184–5
chaat: puffed rice, potato and

chickpea *chaat* **108**,
      109–10
chaat masala 7–8
chai **246**, 247
chakri strips 172, **173**
chana chaat patti 244
chana dhal see chickpeas
chana dhal chaat 110
chana dhal vada 162–3
chapatti flour 16
cheese 17
      cheese and *ajmo* toast 137
      cheesy spinach parcels 126–
            7, **127**
      creamy *paneer* curry **100**,
            101–2
      crispy cheese and potato
            balls **122**, 123
      Indo-Chinese marinated
            cheese stir-fry 152
      Indo-Italian macaroni cheese
            142, 143
      Indo-Italian veggie
            cannelloni 144
      spicy mushroom and pepper
            pizza 150–1
      spicy veggie pie 141
chickpeas 15
      Indian chickpea salad 110
      Indian-style 'falafel' in
            toasted pitta 162–3
      lentil dough ball curry 96–7
      puffed rice, potato and
            chickpea *chaat* **108**,
            109–10
      tangy chickpea salsa 244
      see also gram flour
chikkudu ginjalu see broad beans
chikoo/chico fruit 16
      Indian fruit salad **194**, 195
chillies 8, 26–7
      chilli *paneer* 152
      chillies with sweet cumin
            satay **242**, 243
      garlic and red chilli chutney
            236, 239
      green chilli pizza toast 137
      mashed potato and chilli
            sandwich **112**, 113
      sticky chilli chips 225
chips:
      crispy okra chips **222**, 223
      masala chips 224

sticky chilli chips 225
chora 62
chora fari 176, 177–8
chutney:
      apple and pea chutney **236**,
            238
      garlic and red chilli chutney
            236, 239
      sweet and tangy tamarind
            chutney **236**, 241
cinnamon 8
cloves 8
coconut 26, 29
      mustard seed, curry leaf and
            coconut dip 235, **236**
      spicy coconut peas 131
      sweet and tangy fried rolls
            180–1
coriander 8, 26
      bottle gourd and coriander
            dumplings 52–3
      vegetable patties in
            coriander, garlic and
            tomato sauce 184–5
cornflour 16
cornmeal flatbread 202, **204–5**
courgettes:
      courgette and spinach parcels
            92, **93–4**, 95
      Indo-Italian veggie lasagne
            144
      layered vegetable rice 188–9
      mixed vegetable soup 37
      vegetable rice with mint
            masala **190**, 191
crisps:
      paprika potato crisps 221
      'poppadom' crisps **176**,
            177–8
croquettes: leek, broccoli, spinach
      and asparagus croquettes
      124
cumin 9
      chillies with sweet cumin
            satay **242**, 243
      cumin-infused rice 214–15
      roasting seeds 27, 28
curry leaves 9
      mustard seed, curry leaf and
            coconut dip 235, **236**

D

dabeli **112**, **113**

dhal 28, 228–9
dhal bhati & churma 186–7
dhal fry **70**, 71–2
dhudi bataka rassa **38**, 39
dips:
>   apple and pea chutney **236**, 238
>   garlic and red chilli chutney **236**, 239
>   mustard seed, curry leaf and coconut dip 235, **236**
>   red pepper and carrot relish **236**, 237
>   sweet carrot pickle 233, **236**
>   sweet and tangy tamarind chutney **236**, 241
dosa 16
dough balls:
>   Indo-Chinese street-style rice and noodles 153, **154**, 155
>   lentil dough ball curry 96–7
>   Manchurian cabbage dough balls with vegetable stir-fry 158–9, **159**
>   Rajasthani dough ball curry 98–9
dudhi na muthiya 52–3
dum aloo 90
dum biryani 188–9
dumplings:
>   bottle gourd and coriander dumplings 52–3
>   lentil soup with sweet and savoury dumplings 186–7
>   steamed dumplings 88

E
enchiladas: Indo-Mexican veggie enchiladas 161

F
fansi 50, **51**
falafel: Indian-style 'falafel' in toasted pitta 162–3
fennel seeds 9
fenugreek 9
>   curried fresh fenugreek and potatoes **76**, 77
>   fenugreek flatbread 203, **204–5**
>   fenugreek- and garlic-infused

spinach curry 54, **55**
flatbreads:
>   fenugreek flatbread 203, **204–5**
>   fluffy fried fermented bread 204–5, 208–9
>   healthy cornmeal flatbread 202, **204–5**
>   traditional puffed flatbread 204–5, 206–7
French beans:
>   hot and spicy stir-fry soup 160
>   Indo-Chinese fried rice 157
>   layered vegetable rice 188–9
>   spicy veggie pie 141
>   tomato, carom and French bean curry 50, **51**
>   vegetable *korma* 89
>   vegetable rice with mint masala **190**, 191
fruit salad **194**, 195
fruit salts 16

G
garam masala 9, 12
garlic 12, 26
>   fenugreek- and garlic-infused spinach curry 54, **55**
>   garlic and red chilli chutney **236**, 239
>   vegetable patties in coriander, garlic and tomato sauce 184–5
gatta: Rajasthani *gatta* 98–9
ghee 16
ginger 12
>   saffron and ginger panna cotta **164**, 165
googra 192–3
gourds 15, 20
>   aromatic vegetable and lentil soup 230, **231**, 232
>   bottle gourd and coriander dumplings 52–3
>   pointed gourd and potato curry 82
>   stuffed bitter melon satay 80–1
gram flour 15
>   green pigeon pea and gram flour *bhajis* 120–1
grapes: Indian fruit salad **194**, 195

gur 17

H
hakka noodles 156
Hyderabadi *biryani* **190**, 191

I
idli flour 16
>   *idli sambar* 88
>   *uttapam* **84**, 85
imli see tamarind

J
jaggery 17
jeera baath 214–15
juvar/jowar 17

K
kakadhia 179
kakra bhajia 27, 221
karella na reveya 80–1
khanda bataka 48
khaskahas/khuskhus see poppy seeds
khudi 226–7
kidney beans: Punjabi-style kidney bean curry 60, **61**
kobi pura 36
kofta: vegetable *kofta* 184–5
kopru 235, **236**
korma: vegetable *korma* 89
kurmura see puffed rice

L
lasagne: Indo-Italian veggie lasagne 144
lasan bhaji 54, **55**
lasan chutney **236**, 239
leek, broccoli, spinach and asparagus croquettes 124
lentils 22, 27
>   aromatic vegetable and lentil soup 230, **231**, 232
>   lentil dough ball curry 96–7
>   lentil soup with sweet and savoury dumplings 186–7
>   spicy lentil curry **70**, 71–2
>   traditional yellow lentil soup 228–9
loht 16

M
macaroni cheese **142**, 143

makai cutlets 118, **119**
makai khanda vada 117
makai no loht/makki ka atta 16
makai rotla 202, **204–5**
mamra see puffed rice
Manchow soup 160
Manchurian cabbage dough balls
　　with vegetable stir-fry
　　158–9, **159**
mangoes 16
　　puffed rice, potato and
　　　　chickpea *chaat* 108,
　　　　109–10
marrows: creamy marrow and
　　potato soup 38, 39
masala chai 246, 247
masala chips 224
mausami tikki 124
methi bhaji bataka **76**, 77
milk pudding 196–7
milo flour 17
mint: vegetable rice with mint
　　masala **190**, 191
mitu gajar murabho 233
momra see puffed rice
Mumbai sandwich 40
mung/moong 17
　　green *mung* bean curry 73
　　spiced sprouted *mung* beans
　　　　78, **79**
mung dhal/moong dhal 17, 73
mung vadhu 78, **79**
mushrooms:
　　Indo-Chinese street food
　　　　noodles 156
　　Indo-Italian veggie
　　　　cannelloni 144
　　Indo-Italian veggie lasagne
　　　　144
　　spicy mushroom and pepper
　　　　pizza 150–1
　　spicy veggie pie 141
mushy pea soup with potato
　　patties 74–5
mustard seeds 12–13
　　mustard seed, curry leaf and
　　　　coconut dip 235, **236**

N
noodles:
　　Indo-Chinese street food
　　　　noodles 156
　　Indo-Chinese street-style rice

and noodles 153,
　　154, 155
　　see also vermicelli
nuts:
　　spiced nut parcels 192–3
　　see also specific nuts

O
okra 15
　　crispy okra chips **222**, 223
onions:
　　cumin-infused rice 214–15
　　potato and onion curry 48
　　south Indian mixed vegetable
　　　　pancake **84**, 85
　　sweetcorn and onion *bhajis*
　　　　117
　　vegetable *korma* 89

P
palak & paneer googra 126–7,
　　127
palak puri 218, 219–20
pancakes:
　　cabbage pancakes 36
　　south Indian mixed vegetable
　　　　pancakes **84**, 85
paneer 17
　　cheesy spinach parcels 126–
　　　　7, **127**
　　creamy *paneer* curry **100**,
　　　　101–2
　　griddled pepper and *paneer*
　　　　69
　　Indo-Chinese marinated
　　　　cheese stir-fry 152
　　paneer ravioli 147–8, **149**
　　paneer spheres **122**, 123
　　shredded *paneer* curry 56
paneer & mattar bhurgi 56
paneer tikka 69
panna cotta **164**, 165
papdi lilva see broad beans
paprika potato crisps 221
parvar/parval/parwal see gourds
patra 20
　　turai patra 92, 93–4, **95**
pauwa/pawa/poha 20
pav bhaji 68
pav bhaji masala powder 13
pav vada 114
peanuts:
　　chillies with sweet cumin

satay **242**, 243
　　Kaushy's Bombay mix
　　　　174–5
　　sweet and tangy fried rolls
　　　　180–1
　　tapioca, peanut and potato
　　　　bhajis 116
　　vine tomato satay **44**, 45–6
pears: Indian fruit salad **194**, 195
peas 27
　　apple and pea chutney **236**,
　　　　238
　　aromatic vegetable and lentil
　　　　soup 230, **231**, 232
　　cabbage and pea curry 57
　　Indo-Chinese fried rice 157
　　Indo-Italian macaroni cheese
　　　　142, 143
　　layered vegetable rice 188–9
　　mashed vegetable curry rolls
　　　　68
　　mushy pea soup with potato
　　　　patties 74–5
　　savoury Indian porridge 42,
　　　　43
　　soya mince and pea curry 63
　　spiced potato and pea toastie
　　　　40
　　spicy coconut peas 131
　　spicy pea and potato pasties
　　　　140
　　spicy veggie burgers **138**,
　　　　139
　　vegetable *korma* 89
　　vegetable patties in
　　　　coriander, garlic and
　　　　tomato sauce 184–5
pepper 13
peppers 26
　　griddled pepper and *paneer*
　　　　69
　　hot and spicy stir-fry soup
　　　　160
　　Indo-Chinese fried rice 157
　　Indo-Chinese street food
　　　　noodles 156
　　Indo-Chinese street-style rice
　　　　and noodles 153,
　　　　154, 155
　　Indo-Italian macaroni cheese
　　　　142, 143
　　Indo-Italian veggie lasagne
　　　　144

layered vegetable rice 188–9
Manchurian cabbage dough balls with vegetable stir-fry 158–9, **159**
mixed vegetable soup 37
pepper and sweetcorn curry **58**, 59
red pepper and carrot relish **236**, 237
savoury Indian porridge 42, **43**
south Indian mixed vegetable pancake 84, 85
spicy mushroom and pepper pizza 150–1
spicy veggie burgers **138**, 139
pies: spicy veggie pie 141
pigeon peas 22, 27
    aromatic vegetable and lentil soup 230, **231**, 232
    green pigeon pea and gram flour *bhajis* 120–1
    pigeon pea rice 212
    pigeon peas and rice **216**, 217
pilau:
    tameta pilau **210**, 211
    tuvar pilau 212
pistachios: spiced nut parcels 192–3
pitta breads: Indian-style 'falafel' in toasted pitta 162–3
pizza:
    pizza toast 137
    spicy mushroom and pepper pizza 150–1
pointed gourd 20
    pointed gourd and potato curry 82
pomegranate: Indian fruit salad **194**, 195
'poppadom' crisps **176**, 177–8
poppy seeds 22
    vegetable rice with mint masala **190**, 191
porridge: savoury Indian porridge 42, **43**
potatoes 28
    bay leaf infused new potato curry 90
    creamy marrow and potato soup 38, **39**

crispy cheese and potato balls **122**, 123
crispy rice and potato snacks 172, **173**
curried fresh fenugreek and potatoes **76**, 77
Gujarati mixed vegetable pot 182, **183**
Indian fried bread 111
Indo-Italian macaroni cheese **142**, 143
kakra bhajia 27
Kaushy's Bombay mix 174–5
mashed potato and chilli sandwich 112, **113**
mashed vegetable curry rolls 68
massala chips 224
mushy pea soup with potato patties 74–5
paprika potato crisps 221
pointed gourd and potato curry 82
potato and onion curry 48
potato and tomato curry 47
puffed rice, potato and chickpea *chaat* **108**, 109–10
spiced potato and pea toastie 40
spicy bread and potato patties 114
spicy pea and potato pasties 140
spicy veggie burgers **138**, 139
spicy veggie pie 141
sticky chilli chips 225
tapioca, peanut and potato *bhajis* 116
puffed rice 17
    puffed rice, potato and chickpea *chaat* **108**, 109–10
Punjabi-style kidney bean curry 60, **61**
puri: palak puri **218**, 219–20

R
ragdah pethis 74–5
Rajasthani dough ball curry 98–9
rajma 60, **61**

ratalu see yams
ravioli: *paneer* ravioli 147–8, **149**
red peppers *see* peppers
renghan bharta 86
renghan lothiu 34, **35**
rice 15, 17, 20, 27
    boiled basmati rice 213
    crispy rice and potato snacks 172, **173**
    cumin-infused rice 214–15
    fluffy tomato rice **210**, 211
    Indo-Chinese fried rice 157
    Indo-Chinese street-style rice and noodles 153, **154**, 155
    layered vegetable rice 188–9
    pigeon pea rice 212
    pigeon peas and rice **216**, 217
    puffed rice, potato and chickpea *chaat* **108**, 109–10
    vegetable rice with mint masala **190**, 191
rice flour 20
ricotta cheese: Indo-Italian veggie cannelloni 144
rolls:
    mashed vegetable curry rolls 68
    sweet and tangy fried rolls 180–1
rotla: makai rotla 202, **204–5**
rotli **204–5**, 206–7

S
sabudana 20
sabudana kichdi 41
sabudana vada 116
sabzhi rassa 37
sabzi & paneer makni **100**, 101–2
safarjan wattana **236**, 238
saffron and ginger panna cotta **164**, 165
sakabhaji upma 42, **43**
salsa: tangy chickpea salsa 244
salt: Indian black salt 12
sambar 230, **231**, 232
    idli sambar 88
sandwiches:
    mashed potato and chilli sandwich 112, **113**

Mumbai sandwich 40
sapodilla *see chikoo*/chico fruit
satay:
    chillies with sweet cumin
        satay **242, 243**
    stuffed bitter melon satay
        80–1
    vine tomato satay **44**, 45–6
semolina 20
    savoury Indian porridge 42,
        43
    semolina-encrusted
        sweetcorn *bhajis* 118,
        119
sev 20, 197
sev momra/sev mamra 20
sev momra bhel **108**, 109–10
shimla makai 58, **59**
shimla mirch **236**, 237
soji/sooji see semolina
sorghum flour 17
soups:
    aromatic vegetable and lentil
        soup 230, **231**, 232
    creamy marrow and potato
        soup **38, 39**
    hot and spicy stir-fry soup
        160
    lentil soup with sweet and
        savoury dumplings
        186–7
    mixed vegetable soup 37
    mushy pea soup with potato
        patties 74–5
    spiced yoghurt soup 226–7
    traditional yellow lentil soup
        228–9
soya mince and pea curry 63
spices 7–13, 27
    see also specific spices
spinach:
    cheesy spinach parcels 126–
        7, **127**
    courgette and spinach parcel
        92, 93–4, **95**
    fenugreek- and garlic-infused
        spinach curry 54, **55**
    Indo-Italian veggie
        cannelloni 144
    leek, broccoli, spinach and
        asparagus croquettes
        124
    spinach 'clouds' **218**, 219–20

steamed dumplings 88
stir-fry:
    hot and spicy stir-fry soup
        160
    Indo-Chinese marinated
        cheese stir-fry 152
    Manchurian cabbage dough
        balls with vegetable
        stir-fry 158–9, **159**
stuffed bitter melon satay 80–1
sukhu kobi wattana 57
sukhu parvar bataka 82
sweet potatoes: Gujarati mixed
    vegetable pot 182, **183**
sweetcorn:
    mixed vegetable soup 37
    pepper and sweetcorn curry
        58, **59**
    semolina-encrusted
        sweetcorn *bhajis* 118,
        119
    sweetcorn and onion *bhajis*
        117
Szechuan rice 157

T

tamarind 16–17
    sweet and tangy tamarind
        chutney **236**, 241
tameta pilau **210**, 211
tameta reveya **44**, 45–6
tapioca 20
    spiced savoury tapioca 41
    tapioca, peanut and potato
        bhajis 116
tarka/tadka 22, 29
tawa 22
tea: spicy tea **246**, 247
toast: green chilli pizza toast 137
toasties: spiced potato and pea
    toastie 40
tomatoes 27
    aromatic vegetable and lentil
        soup 230, **231**, 232
    fluffy tomato rice **210**, 211
    potato and tomato curry 47
    south Indian mixed vegetable
        pancakes **84**, 85
    tomato, carom and French
        bean curry 50, **51**
    vegetable patties in
        coriander, garlic and
        tomato sauce 184–5

vine tomato satay **44**, 45–6
tortillas:
    Indo-Mexican veggie
        enchiladas 161
    spicy yoghurty tortillas 128,
        129
turai patra **92**, 93–4, **95**
turmeric 13
    spiced yoghurt soup 226–7
tuvar/toor see pigeon peas
tuvar dhal/toor dhal 22
tuvar dhal kichdi **216**, 217
tuvar dhokri vada 120–1
tuvar pilau 212

U

undhiyu 182, **183**
urad dhal/urid dhal 22
urad/urid flour 22
uttapam **84**, 85

V

vagarela tortillas 128, **129**
vagarela wattana 131
vagarela beans 136
vermicelli 20
    sweet cardamom vermicelli
        197

Y

yams 20
    Gujarati mixed vegetable pot
        182, **183**
yoghurt 26, 29
    mustard seed, curry leaf and
        coconut dip 235, **236**
    spiced yoghurt soup 226–7
    spicy yoghurty tortillas 128,
        129

First published in Great Britain in 2015 by Saltyard Books
An imprint of Hodder & Stoughton
An Hachette UK company

1

The tiles on pages 58, 204–5 and 236 were provided by
Fired Earth www.firedearth.com / 0845 366 0400

The background papers on pages 35, 51, 54, 84, 142 and 218
were provided by Dandelion Tree www.dandeliontree.co.uk

A CIP catalogue record for this title is available from the British Library.

ISBN 978 1 444 73474 4
eBook ISBN 978 1 444 73476 8

Book design by Ami Smithson at cabinlondon.co.uk
Typeset in Sabon and Burford

Copy editors Bryony Nowell and Laura Herring
Proof reader Annie Lee
Indexer Caroline Wilding
Food stylist Ellie Jarvis
Prop stylist Lydia Brun

Printed and bound in Germany by Mohn Media

Hodder & Stoughton policy is to use papers that are natural, renewable and
recyclable products and made from wood grown in sustainable forests.
The logging and manufacturing processes are expected to conform to the
environmental regulations of the country of origin.

Saltyard Books
Carmelite House
50 Victoria Embankment
London EC4Y 0DZ

www.saltyardbooks.co.uk